DEAD ON NINE

by Jack Popplewell

Copyright © 1956 by Jack Popplewell
All Rights Reserved

DEAD ON NINE is fully protected under the copyright laws of the British Commonwealth, including Canada, the United States of America, and all other countries of the Copyright Union. All rights, including professional and amateur stage productions, recitation, lecturing, public reading, motion picture, radio broadcasting, television, online/digital production, and the rights of translation into foreign languages are strictly reserved.

ISBN 978-0-573-01092-7

concordtheatricals.co.uk
concordtheatricals.com

FOR AMATEUR PRODUCTION ENQUIRIES

UNITED KINGDOM AND WORLD
EXCLUDING NORTH AMERICA
licensing@concordtheatricals.co.uk
020-7054-7298

Each title is subject to availability from Concord Theatricals,
depending upon country of performance.

CAUTION: Professional and amateur producers are hereby warned that *DEAD ON NINE* is subject to a licensing fee. The purchase, renting, lending or use of this book does not constitute a licence to perform this title(s), which licence must be obtained from the appropriate agent prior to any performance. Performance of this title(s) without a licence is a violation of copyright law and may subject the producer and/or presenter of such performances to penalties. Both amateurs and professionals considering a production are strongly advised to apply to the appropriate agent before starting rehearsals, advertising, or booking a theatre. A licensing fee must be paid whether the title is presented for charity or gain and whether or not admission is charged.

This work is published by Samuel French, an imprint of Concord Theatricals Ltd.

The Professional Rights in this play are controlled by Vertriebsstelle und Verlag Buchweizenkoppel 19, 22844 Norderstedt, Germany.

No one shall make any changes in this title for the purpose of production. No part of this book may be reproduced, stored in a retrieval system, scanned, uploaded, or transmitted in any form, by any means, now known or yet to be invented, including mechanical, electronic, digital, photocopying, recording, videotaping, or otherwise, without the prior written permission of the publisher. No one shall share this title, or part of this title, to any social media or file hosting websites.

The moral right of Jack Popplewell to be identified as author of this work has been asserted in accordance with Section 77 of the Copyright, Designs and Patents Act 1988.

USE OF COPYRIGHTED MUSIC

A licence issued by Concord Theatricals to perform this play does not include permission to use the incidental music specified in this publication. In the United Kingdom: Where the place of performance is already licensed by the PERFORMING RIGHT SOCIETY (PRS) a return of the music used must be made to them. If the place of performance is not so licensed then application should be made to PRS for Music (www.prsformusic.com). A separate and additional licence from PHONOGRAPHIC PERFORMANCE LTD (www.ppluk.com) may be needed whenever commercial recordings are used. Outside the United Kingdom: Please contact the appropriate music licensing authority in your territory for the rights to any incidental music.

USE OF COPYRIGHTED THIRD-PARTY MATERIALS

Licensees are solely responsible for obtaining formal written permission from copyright owners to use copyrighted third-party materials (e.g., artworks, logos) in the performance of this play and are strongly cautioned to do so. If no such permission is obtained by the licensee, then the licensee must use only original materials that the licensee owns and controls. Licensees are solely responsible and liable for clearances of all third-party copyrighted materials, and shall indemnify the copyright owners of the play(s) and their licensing agent, Concord Theatricals Ltd., against any costs, expenses, losses and liabilities arising from the use of such copyrighted third-party materials by licensees.

IMPORTANT BILLING AND CREDIT REQUIREMENTS

If you have obtained performance rights to this title, please refer to your licensing agreement for important billing and credit requirements.

DEAD ON NINE

Presented by James P. Sherwood at the Westminster Theatre, London, on the 24th August, 1955, with the following cast of characters:

(in the order of their appearance)

TOM HAMMOND	*Maurice Kaufmann*
ROBERT LEIGH	*Griffith Jones*
MARION DALE	*Jean Lodge*
ESMERALDA LEIGH, Robert's wife	*Hy Hazell*
RICHARD FARROW	*Andrew Cruickshank*
GLADYS, the maid	*Gabrielle Hamilton*
LESLIE BOOTH	*Anthony Snell*

The play directed by GEOFFREY WARDWELL

Setting designed by GEOFFREY GHIN

SYNOPSIS OF SCENES

The action of the play passes in the living-room of the Leighs' week-end cottage at Hambledon, a fishing village on the South Coast of England

ACT I

SCENE 1 A September afternoon
SCENE 2 The following day. Early afternoon
SCENE 3 Two o'clock the following morning

ACT II

SCENE 1 Ten a.m. the same day
SCENE 2 Two days later. Early afternoon

ACT III

SCENE 1 The next morning
SCENE 2 Evening of the same day

Time—the present

To face page 1—Dead on Nine

Photograph by Houston Rogers

DEAD ON NINE

ACT I

Scene i

SCENE—*The living-room of the Leighs' week-end cottage at Hambledon, a fishing village on the South Coast of England. A September afternoon.*
It is a light airy room, suggesting its proximity to farmlands and the sea. There is a door to the garden and road up C, *a door* L *to the kitchen and other parts of the house and a door to Esmeralda's bedroom* R. *A wide window across the corner up* R *has a built-in seat and gives a view of the garden with a wide expanse of sky beyond. The fireplace is down* R. *A baby grand piano, a desk, a sofa, two easy chairs and a radiogram are the main pieces of furniture. There is a cupboard for drinks down* L. *A telephone stands on the left end of the piano. A large clock hangs prominently on the wall up* C. *At night the room is lit by wall-brackets, and table-lamps on the mantelpiece and piano. The light switch is* L *of the door up* C.
(*See the Ground Plan and Photograph of the Scene*)

When the CURTAIN *rises, it is a fine sunny afternoon. There is some wind and from time to time the sound of the surf is heard.* ROBERT LEIGH *is seated at the desk, scanning the typewritten pages of a manuscript.* TOM HAMMOND *is standing by the window, his hands in the pockets of his riding-breeches.*

ROBERT. What did you say?
TOM. I said "The two most beautiful and high-spirited animals God created are women and horses."
ROBERT (*vaguely*) You're probably right.
TOM. I am right.
ROBERT. Which do you prefer?
TOM. I can't get along without either of 'em.
ROBERT. It's a nuisance, isn't it?

(*There is a pause*)

I suppose you stayed the night with her?
TOM. Sure I did.
ROBERT (*absent-mindedly*) She's a beauty.
TOM. She certainly is.

(MARION DALE *enters* L. *She is wearing horn-rimmed spectacles*)

MARION (*crossing to* L *of the desk*) Are you ready, Mr Leigh?
ROBERT. Nearly. I'm on the last page. (*To* Tom) Did you have

to spend the night with her yourself? Couldn't somebody else have done it?

TOM. I don't trust anybody else.

ROBERT. I see your point.

MARION (*moving a little up* C) Is this a very private conversation?

TOM. Good heavens, no.

ROBERT (*laughing*) We're talking about a horse.

MARION. Oh!

TOM. She's just presented me with a foal.

MARION. So you slept with her?

TOM. In the stable. Me and the vet.

MARION. I see.

TOM (*to Marion*) You thought . . .

ROBERT (*to Marion*) I found one or two little errors, Marion.

(MARION *moves to* L *of Robert*)

(*He points to the manuscript*) It's "lonely widow", not "lovely widow".

MARION (*looking at the manuscript*) Sorry.

ROBERT. If she was lovely she wouldn't be lonely, would she?

MARION. She might. If she was faithful, I mean.

ROBERT. If she's a widow she's no-one to be faithful to.

MARION. There are such things as memories.

ROBERT (*dryly*) Yes, dear, I know. Here's a spelling error. How do you spell "receive"?

MARION. R-E-C-E-I-V-E.

(TOM *moves down* R)

ROBERT. No. I before E except after C.

MARION. It is after C.

ROBERT. What? Oh, yes. (*He coughs and smiles*) There are one or two other little things I've marked. Will you alter them?

MARION. Yes.

ROBERT. Oh, where's my pen?

(MARION *crosses above Robert to* R *of him. They search for the pen on the desk.* MARION *finds the pen and hands it to* ROBERT *who writes a couple of words on the manuscript*)

I always lose pens. I blame my ears.

TOM. What the hell have your ears got to do with it?

ROBERT. Everybody but me seems capable of sticking a pen behind his ear. I can't. It always falls off. It's a grave handicap.

TOM (*to Marion*) He's crazy.

MARION (*without sympathy*) Yes. Isn't he?

ROBERT (*handing the manuscript to Marion*) Thanks, Marion.

(MARION *crosses above Robert towards the door* L)

Where's Esmeralda?

MARION (*pausing and turning* LC) She went with the Howards to the harbour.
TOM. Howard's painting his boat. He likes an audience when he works. Well, he's an actor, isn't he?

(MARION *exits* L)

What's this you're writing? A new play?
ROBERT. Yes. A murder melodrama. I finished the second act last night.
TOM. Is it good?
ROBERT. No.
TOM (*moving to the sofa*) I'll say one thing for you, Robert. (*He sits on the sofa at the upstage end*) You're honest.
ROBERT. I'm not honest in the least. I'm candid.
TOM. Beats me how authors keep on thinking up new ideas.
ROBERT. I hate to admit it, but it beats me, too.
TOM. What do you do—write it all out in longhand, or do you dictate it?
ROBERT. I've tried dictation, I've tried tape-recording, but it cramps my style. I write it in longhand and my secretary types it. (*He concentrates on his papers, hand to head*)
TOM (*glancing towards the door* L) She's all right, isn't she?
ROBERT. Who?
TOM. Your secretary.
ROBERT. She's very efficient.
TOM (*laughing*) Yes? Who's kidding who?
ROBERT. I don't think I get you.
TOM. Oh, no?
ROBERT. You're right. I do get you. You sleep with your horse. You imply that I share a stall with my secretary. I don't. (*He rises, crosses to the radiogram down* L *and picks up an opened bottle of beer that is standing on it*)
TOM. My God, you're touchy all of a sudden.
ROBERT (*smiling*) Sorry.
TOM. You're a contradictory sort of person, Robert. I never quite understand you.
ROBERT (*crossing to the desk*) I don't understand you. (*He pours some beer into the two tankards on the desk*)
TOM. I'm easy enough to get to know.
ROBERT. Conversationally, yes. (*He stands the bottle on the desk*) You're the kind of man who can walk into a bar parlour and get pally with everybody in five minutes flat. (*He passes a tankard to Tom*)
TOM. So are you.
ROBERT. No. It'd take me ten minutes. I don't understand your being a farmer. I should have thought your talents lay in other directions.

Tom. Such as what?

Robert. I don't know.

Tom. It's only forty acres. I like horses—so I can ride. It's by the coast and I like boats. So I can ride, and I can sail.

Robert. What more do you want?

Tom. Oh, I don't know. I'd like to be rich.

Robert (*sitting in the desk chair*) Aren't you?

Tom. Are you kidding?

Robert. Most of us can only afford to spend week-ends here. You're here all the time.

Tom. Yes, working like a black. I've got a farm, not an office in town. As a matter of fact, I'm damned hard up. Could you lend me ten thousand pounds? I'm expecting a postal order.

Robert. You'd better ask Esmeralda. I'm a playwright.

Tom. Esmeralda? Rich?

Robert. She admits it. She is not ashamed of it. Her father had about a hundred thousand acres of sheep in Australia. She'll tell you.

Tom (*rising and moving to the fireplace*) They say the rich never go to heaven. They don't have to, they're there already.

Robert. I see what you mean. How long have you had this farm?

Tom. Six months. I was over here during the war and when I left the Canadian Army I came back.

Robert. I thought Canada offered good prospects for farming.

Tom. The best. There was also a girl.

Robert. Oh!

Tom. She already had a husband. (*He drains his tankard*)

Robert. So you couldn't be married?

Tom (*moving to R of the desk*) Who said I wanted to be married? (*He puts his tankard on the desk*) She was attractive. I like women. I like lots of 'em, but one at a time.

Robert (*rising*) My hobby's writing plays. (*He picks up the two tankards and the bottle, crosses and puts them on the radiogram*)

Tom (*turning to the window*) You can keep it. (*He glances off*) Here's your wife.

Robert (*moving to the piano*) Are the Howards with her? (*He takes a cigarette from the box on the piano*)

Tom. No. She's a very attractive woman. You sure writing plays is your only interest in life?

Robert. My major interest. (*He lights his cigarette*) Unfortunately it isn't self-supporting. Esmeralda is.

Tom. Hey, wait a minute now. Are you telling me you married Esmeralda for her money?

Robert (*ironically*) What an immoral suggestion.

(Esmeralda Leigh *enters up* c. *She carries her handbag. She glances at Robert but speaks only to Tom*)

ESMERALDA (*moving above the desk*) Hello, Tom, the sea's wonderful and there's a heavenly breeze. The Haslemeres are sailing close to the rocks again.
ROBERT. Silly young fools.
ESMERALDA. Joe Howard's painting his boat.
TOM. Yes?
ESMERALDA. Yes. (*To Robert*) Did you finish the play?
ROBERT. The second act.
ESMERALDA. How nice! What were you talking about?
TOM. Money.
ESMERALDA. Why?
ROBERT. He's always hated rich idlers and he's always wanted to be one. (*He crosses to the cupboard down* L *and fills his cigarette case from the box in the cupboard*)
ESMERALDA (*to Tom*) Is that your ambition in life?
TOM. One of them.
ROBERT. The other is women.
ESMERALDA. You're fond of the ladies, are you?
TOM. What man isn't?
ESMERALDA. I'd no idea Tom was romantic. (*She turns to Robert*) Had you, Robert?
ROBERT. I hadn't given it a great deal of thought.
ESMERALDA. But you should. (*She moves to* L *of Tom*) Yes. Yes, you are the romantic type, aren't you? I imagine you could be pretty ruthless if ever you wanted to, couldn't you?

(*The sound of the surf fades*)

TOM. I don't know. I've never had to be.
ESMERALDA. But you could. Why have you never married, Tom?
TOM. I never saw the woman I'd trust with an anchor and chain.
ESMERALDA. But if ever you do?
TOM. If she's what I'm looking for I'd give her the anchor and tell her to heave it overboard.
ESMERALDA. Providing she fulfils all the necessary specifications?

(ROBERT *moves to the piano*)

TOM. She can have the moon on a silver platter.
ROBERT. You haven't got the moon on a silver platter.
TOM (*moving down* R) I'd get it.

(*There is a pause*)

ESMERALDA (*smiling*) Robert expects his women to give *him* the moon. He provides the platter, of course.
ROBERT (*angrily*) That was a charming thing to say.
ESMERALDA. Yes, wasn't it. (*To Tom*) Deep down we're devoted

to each other. By the way, the Tyrrells are throwing a little party. They asked us to drop in for cocktails. (*To Robert*) I said we would.

ROBERT (*moving to the desk chair*) You take Tom. I'll come later. (*He sits*)

ESMERALDA. How much later?

ROBERT. Five or ten minutes. (*He studies his manuscript*)

ESMERALDA (*to Tom*) Will you go?

TOM. Sure. I'd love to.

ESMERALDA (*to Tom*) I saw Dick Farrow on my way back.

(ROBERT *looks up*)

He's going to the party.

TOM. The Chief Constable himself.

ESMERALDA. Why do you call him that?

TOM. He's so damned pompous. He's the Canadian's idea of what an English Chief Constable looks like.

ESMERALDA. He isn't quite a Chief Constable, you know. Why don't you like him?

TOM. Who says I don't?

ROBERT. Perhaps you're prejudiced because he's a policeman.

TOM (*with a step towards Robert*) Why did you say that?

ROBERT. What did I say?

TOM. You said I don't like policemen.

ROBERT. Some people don't. Do you?

TOM. I don't give a damn about them.

ROBERT. Then that's all right.

(*There is a rather uncomfortable silence*)

ESMERALDA. He said he'd call in on his way to the Tyrrells if he had time. He's been out fishing. He said he'd leave us a couple of trout.

ROBERT. Good.

TOM (*moving to the door up* C) I think I'll go and start the car.

(TOM *exits up* C, *leaving the door open*)

ESMERALDA. Are you coming to the party?

(*The light begins to fade as the sun starts to set*)

ROBERT. I said I'd be ready in five or ten minutes.

ESMERALDA. I know you did. It occurred to me that that was probably an excuse to stay behind.

ROBERT. Would that cause you any despondency?

ESMERALDA. No.

ROBERT. Then why discuss it?

ESMERALDA. People might ask if you're to be expected. It's nice to be able to answer them.

ROBERT. I see.

ESMERALDA (*moving up* C) How long has Tom Hammond been here?
ROBERT. Half an hour.
ESMERALDA. Why did he come?
ROBERT. I asked him in.
ESMERALDA. Oh! (*She moves slightly down* C) He's quite a character, isn't he? Attractive.
ROBERT. Do you think so?
ESMERALDA. Why did you ask him in? I shouldn't have thought you'd have much in common.
ROBERT. Mere neighbourliness.
ESMERALDA. Did you think I'd like him?
ROBERT. I didn't consider the possibility.
ESMERALDA. Because I do.
ROBERT (*interested*) Do you?
ESMERALDA. Is that what you hoped?
ROBERT. I don't know what you mean.
ESMERALDA. If you think one of these handsome Romeos is going to persuade me into divorcing you, you're quite, quite mistaken. No, Robert, I won't divorce you.
ROBERT. You're repeating yourself.
ESMERALDA. I want there to be no misunderstanding.
ROBERT. There isn't any.

(MARION *enters* L)

ESMERALDA. Good. (*She moves towards the door up* C, *then stops, turns, takes some notes from her handbag and hands them to* ROBERT) Oh, by the way, there is the money you asked for. (*She moves to the door up* C) Don't forget. I'll see you at the Tyrrells. If Dick brings the trout, put them in the fridge.

(ESMERALDA *exits up* C, *leaving the door open*. ROBERT *rises, pockets the notes, moves to the door up* C *and closes it*. MARION *closes the door* L, *and with her hands behind her on the door knob, she leans back against the door. She and* ROBERT *look at each other in silence for a few moments*)

ROBERT (*moving* C) It must be soon. Do you understand?

(*The sounds of a car departing are heard off*)

MARION (*moving to the piano*) Darling, I do. (*She takes off her spectacles and puts them on the piano*)

(*The lights dim slowly as the sun sets*)

ROBERT. I think she almost enjoys herself. (*He crosses above the desk to the fireplace*) Some people are like that, Marion. They revel in torment. They even glory in their own torment.
MARION. I don't understand her.
ROBERT. How could you? She's laughing deep inside her, but

it's a horrible twisted sort of laughter. She doesn't want me, and she won't let me go. There's something sadistic about it.

MARION. Was she always like that?

ROBERT. Cold? Did you hear what she said? "Put the trout in the fridge." The walls of Jericho can fall—but don't forget to put the trout in the refrigerator.

MARION. Does she know about me?

ROBERT. How can she?

MARION. If she did know, would she care?

ROBERT. Care? Not in normal warm-hearted jealousy—no. But it would hurt her and give her that twisted emotion she enjoys.

MARION. She doesn't want you herself. Why should she mind me?

ROBERT (*crossing to* R *of Marion*) You've no—doubts, have you?

MARION (*grimly*) None.

ROBERT. I mustn't do it. Obviously, I mustn't do it. You do see, don't you?

MARION. We've agreed over that.

ROBERT. Yes. I'd be the first suspect. They'd come down on me like a ton of bricks.

MARION. All the better.

ROBERT. Why?

MARION. If it's—someone else.

ROBERT. But of course I must have that perfect alibi.

MARION. It shouldn't be difficult.

ROBERT. It's easy to have an alibi, but this must be perfect. I don't want to create it, I want it to create itself. I want to fit in with someone else's suggestion, so that later on—after the—so that later on they can't recall that I proposed it.

MARION. But, darling, when?

ROBERT. There's no telling. It isn't something I can force. It's got to happen of its own accord. Now if my agent phoned me to go up to town, or someone fell ill and they sent for me, then it could happen. (*He moves above the desk*) We must wait until it does.

MARION. Are you sure she doesn't know about me?

ROBERT. At least she hasn't the gift of second sight.

MARION (*thoughtfully*) Because if she suspected anything between us she might talk about it.

ROBERT. She can't. God knows we've been careful.

MARION (*glancing away*) Not—very careful.

ROBERT. What do you mean?

MARION. Isn't it obvious—yet?

ROBERT (*moving to* R *of her*) Oh, my darling ... (*He starts to embrace her*)

MARION (*moving quickly away*) Someone may come in. This is another reason it's got to be soon, isn't it?

ROBERT. Yes, it is.
MARION. Because I'll begin to—it'll be obvious. Perhaps it is already?
ROBERT. No. No. You're quite sure?
MARION. Quite sure. (*She pauses*) Bob, how much do you love me?

(ROBERT *moves towards her*)

No. Stay there and tell me.
ROBERT. I—love you, Marion.
MARION. Thank you. That's my only excuse for doing what I'm going to do, you see. It's the only thing that gives me determination to see it through. That makes sense, doesn't it?
ROBERT. I honestly believe it does, my darling. Can you do it?
MARION. I know I can.
ROBERT. It'll take nerve.
MARION. I know. At night in the dark it won't be quite so simple. But no shadows are going to stop me. Believe me.
ROBERT. I do. You won't be suspected, but you'll have to answer the usual routine questions. You have a bungalow on the edge of the wood. I took it so that you could be here at the weekends. Your aunt is staying with you. She goes to bed at ten o'clock and so do you. You don't know anyone around here, so you're not likely to have casual callers dropping in on you. Your aunt won't hear you leave the house and she won't hear you get back. If things go well . . .
MARION. They must.
ROBERT. Yes. Yes, of course. If I've figured out the times correctly—it won't take more than fifteen minutes. This house will be deserted except for Esmeralda.
MARION. You're sure of that?
ROBERT. She will be alone, and in bed. (*He points to the door* R) In there. Say at two o'clock.
MARION. Two o'clock?
ROBERT. At exactly two o'clock. That's important. Those medical folk are pretty clever. They'll know within an hour or so what time it happened.
MARION. How can they tell?
ROBERT. I don't know. But believe me, they can. They'll know the time within a couple of hours and I must be away at that time.
MARION. But the shot?
ROBERT. No-one will hear it.
MARION. Everything depends on that.

(*The sound of the surf is heard*)

ROBERT. That's where a bad thing becomes a good one. This

is the only house we could buy and it's a quarter of a mile from the nearest neighbour. Everybody'll be asleep before two o'clock. It won't be easy.

MARION. I love you, Robert.

ROBERT. Don't do it if you have the slightest doubt, Marion. I wouldn't want you to.

MARION. I'll do it. And then what?

ROBERT (*crossing above the desk to* RC) I'll time it to get back early in the morning. I'll bring someone with me. We'll find Esmeralda.

MARION. Yes.

ROBERT. I'll have a perfect alibi. It couldn't possibly be me. Then I'll get rid of the gun. I'll dump it in the sea. I picked it up cheap in a pub. It's a German revolver. A Luger. No-one could associate it with you or me.

MARION (*moving* LC) And the diamond bracelet. You forgot about the bracelet.

ROBERT. No, I didn't. I shall have taken it with me earlier in the evening.

MARION. You'll say it's missing.

ROBERT. Yes. It will be missing. I'll get rid of it. And it's insured for five thousand pounds. (*He crosses to Marion and takes her hand*) Oh, Marion, if you can only do it. You do realize I'm not merely putting the gun in your hand and then clearing off with an alibi that puts me in safety. Don't you?

MARION. If they catch me they catch us both. That's what you mean, isn't it?

(ROBERT *hesitates a moment then goes to her*)

ROBERT. But they mustn't catch you. They won't. (*He puts his arms about her*) My darling Marion, they can't.

(*The sound of a car arriving is heard off*)

MARION (*breaking from him*) Listen, there is a car. (*She moves to the door up* C, *opens it and glances out*) It's Farrow.

(ROBERT *sits at the piano and plays.* MARION *moves below the piano, picks up her spectacles, puts them on, then goes to* L *of the door up* C)

ROBERT. All right.

(RICHARD FARROW *enters up* C. *He carries two trout on a loop of cord*)

MARION. Come in, Mr Farrow.

FARROW (*moving* C) Hello. Can I interest you in any fish this evening, Miss Dale?

ROBERT. Hello, Dick. I say, they're beauties, aren't they?

Esmeralda gave us strict instructions about them. Give them to Marion.

(MARION *switches on the lights by the switch* L *of the door up* C)

FARROW. They won't bite you.
MARION (*moving to* L *of Farrow*) Are you sure? Don't they look dreadful. (*She shudders as she takes the fish from Farrow*)
FARROW. Oh, I don't know. They're just dead, that's all.

(MARION *crosses to the door* L, *hesitates and turns*)

ROBERT. All right, Marion—put them in the fridge.
MARION. Yes.

(MARION *shivers slightly and exits* L)

FARROW. Did I interrupt you?
ROBERT. Not in the least.
FARROW. Esme said you'd be going to the Tyrrells for drinks.
ROBERT. She went on ahead with young Hammond. I waited for you. (*He rises and crosses to the desk*) I'll just put these away. (*He collects the manuscript together*)

(FARROW *takes a cigarette from his case and crosses easily to the piano*)

FARROW. Have you known Hammond long? (*He lights his cigarette with the lighter on the piano*)
ROBERT. Only this summer.
FARROW. Like him?
ROBERT. I wouldn't trust him too far.
FARROW. He conforms to type. Out of the army. Colonial—restless. Bit of a fly-by-night, I'd say.

(MARION *enters* L *and crosses above the desk to* R *of it*)

ROBERT. Will you take charge of these, Marion? (*He hands her the manuscript. To Robert*) I'm trying to write a play. (*He perches himself on the left end of the desk*) You'd think this was the ideal setting—quiet fishing village and all that sort of thing. Actually it's as hectic as a London night-club.
FARROW (*sitting in the easy chair* LC) It wasn't always so. I was born here. My father paid a few hundreds for the house I've got. The new crowd that's poured in during the last few years has paid thousands for them.
ROBERT. You were born here and you went to London. We're Londoners and we think this is paradise.
FARROW. So do I—for a week-end. What's your play about? Or shouldn't I ask?
ROBERT. Murder melodrama.
FARROW. Why do perfectly kind, law-abiding authors so frequently write about murders?

ROBERT. It's a fascinating subject.

MARION (*crossing to* C) Do you like detective stories? I mean, being a detective yourself.

FARROW. If they're good ones. Of course, they're almost never true to life. Very few people get away with murder.

ROBERT. I'm not so sure about that. (*He rises, takes a cigarette from his case and crosses to the fireplace*) If you read your Sunday paper as thoroughly as I do, you'll come to quite the opposite conclusion. (*He lights his cigarette with the matches on the mantelpiece*)

FARROW. That simply isn't true.

MARION. Do you always get your man?

FARROW. Not always, of course—but I wouldn't risk it if I were you. (*He smiles roguishly*) We'll catch you all right.

(*There is a pause*)

That was supposed to be *funny*.

MARION (*to Robert*) You didn't tell me what to say in reply to the letter from New York.

ROBERT (*crossing to* R *of the desk*) It doesn't matter.

MARION. Shall we leave it for tomorrow?

ROBERT. Yes. Yes, tomorrow.

(MARION *crosses above Farrow to the door* L. *The sound of the surf fades*)

FARROW. Beats me how you write these plays without first-hand experience. If I was writing a play about murder, I'd leave no stone unturned until I'd acquainted myself with my subject.

ROBERT. How?

FARROW. Good lord, you should go along with me. I could take you over the ground, into the house, where a murder has been committed. I could show you the exhibits we piece together. All that sort of thing. It would help you.

ROBERT. Help me? Yes. (*Suddenly thoughtful*) You're right, of course, aren't you? Yes, indeed. I think I *would* like to do that.

(*The exterior lights fade as night falls*)

FARROW. You'd get the atmosphere.

(MARION *exits* L, *taking the manuscript with her. She leaves the door open*)

I know it's a pretty grisly sort of experience. But it *would* be experience.

ROBERT. I'll take you up on that one of these days. (*He crosses to* C) Are you ready for the Tyrrells?

FARROW (*rising and moving to the door up* C) Quite.

ROBERT (*crossing to* LC *and calling*) We're leaving now, Marion.

MARION (*off; calling*) All right.

FARROW. I was just thinking——

ROBERT (*turning*) Yes?
FARROW.—tomorrow . . .
ROBERT. What about it?
FARROW. I'm going up to a place called Milford. It's in Somerset. About a murder.
ROBERT. I've heard of it. Wasn't it mentioned in the papers recently?

(MARION *enters* L)

FARROW (*moving* C) Yes. A girl was found beaten to death. A lonely farm. An old colleague of mine is in charge of the case. He phoned me last night and I promised to travel up to see him. It's a long journey, of course, so you may not care to—but if you'd like to go along with me you're welcome.

(MARION *and* ROBERT *look at each other*)

ROBERT. That's very nice of you.
FARROW. I don't want to persuade you if you don't want to. It's a long train journey. I'd be glad of your company.
ROBERT. How long will it take?
FARROW. I get the ten-thirty train in the morning. If I'm lucky I'll catch one back from Bristol round about ten at night.
ROBERT. We'd be very late back.
FARROW. Yes, that's the snag. Forget it. (*He moves to the door up* C) There'll be something else nearer home.
ROBERT (*quietly*) No. You've whetted my appetite.
FARROW. Really? Splendid!
ROBERT (*to Marion*) Will you make a note of that, Marion? We leave on the ten-thirty train in the morning. I'll be away all day. It's a four hours' run from Bristol, so I'll get back home about—oh—(*he crosses to the window seat*) about half-past two in the morning. (*He collects his scarf from the window seat*)

(MARION *pretends to make a note but writes nothing*)

FARROW. Yes—but you can go home with me when we get back. Then you won't disturb Esmeralda. I'll run you up here after breakfast.
ROBERT (*taking a key from his pocket*) Well, that's a good idea. (*He crosses to the desk, unlocks the drawer and takes out a spare key*)
MARION (*moving* LC *and facing Robert*) I've made a note of it, Mr Leigh.
ROBERT (*handing the spare key to Marion*) Oh, and here is the key of the desk in case you want anything, Marion. (*He locks the drawer and moves up* C. *To Farrow*) Well, shall we go?

FARROW *and* ROBERT *exit up* C *as—*

the CURTAIN *falls*

Scene 2

Scene—*The same. The following day. Early afternoon.*

When the Curtain *rises, it is a sunny afternoon. The table down* R *is now* R *of the sofa. The stage is empty and the telephone is ringing. There is some wind and from time to time the cries of gulls are heard.* Marion *enters* L, *crosses to the telephone on the piano and lifts the receiver.*

Marion (*into the telephone*) Six-o-three . . . No, this is Mr Leigh's secretary . . . Oh, hello . . . No, Mr Leigh isn't in. He caught an early train . . . He's gone to Milford . . . It's somewhere in Somerset . . . Yes, he'll be back late tonight . . . Mrs Leigh? I'll find out. (*She puts down the receiver and moves to* L *of the door up* c)

(Esmeralda *enters up* c. *She has been cutting flowers in the garden and carries a trug basket filled with gladioli*)

Esmeralda. Is it for me? (*She moves to the table* LC *and puts the basket on it*)
Marion. It's Mr Hammond.
Esmeralda. Oh.
Marion. He'd like to speak to you. (*She indicates the basket of flowers*) Shall I put them in water?
Esmeralda. If you will, please.

(Marion *picks up the basket and exits* L)

(*She moves to the piano and picks up the receiver. Into the telephone; with very faint coyness*) Good afternoon, Mr Hammond . . . He's gone with Dick Farrow in search of Atmosphere . . . It's what authors go in search of. It's very important to them . . . They get it off their Income Tax . . . Tonight? . . . I'm going to the village hall. Everybody's going to the village hall . . . There's a wonderful band. Harmonium, fiddle and drums. We do barn dances and things like that. Why not go? . . . I'd love to, but the Howards are calling for me . . . Now? . . . This afternoon? . . . Yes, there is a good breeze . . . Well, if you like. Will you pick me up here? . . . About ten minutes . . . All right . . . 'Bye.

(Esmeralda *replaces the receiver, crosses and exits* R.
Marion *enters* L. *She carries a vase of gladioli. She crosses above the desk and puts the vase on the table* R *of the sofa.*
Esmeralda *enters* R. *She carries a scarf. The wind fades*)

(*She crosses to the sofa*) I'm going with Tom Hammond for a sail. (*She puts the scarf on the back of the sofa*)

(Marion *crosses to* LC)

It's a leaky old tub. It ought to be fun if it doesn't go to the bottom.

MARION. They say he handles it well.
ESMERALDA. I imagine he'll do most things well—wouldn't you?
MARION. Well, I . . . Yes, I suppose he might.
ESMERALDA. Why are you working today? Why don't you take advantage of the boss's absence and get out into the fresh air? (*She sits on the sofa, takes her compact from her handbag on the seat beside her and attends to her make-up*)
MARION. Mr Leigh wanted me to catch up with everything whilst he's away.
ESMERALDA. I see. Is it awful being a secretary, Miss Dale?
MARION. It's one way of earning a living.
ESMERALDA. I hope I'm not being rude, but those glasses—are they necessary?
MARION. My eyes are rather weak.
ESMERALDA. But I've seen you without them.
MARION. They're for—reading.
ESMERALDA. I thought you would say that. But one day I called in at the village library and saw you there. You weren't wearing them. And you were reading.
MARION. Was I?
ESMERALDA. You looked very beautiful. Perhaps you think they make you look more learned—more as an efficient secretary should look?
MARION. I'd better go back to my typewriter.
ESMERALDA. No, don't go. I never had to work for a living. I suppose I'm lucky, but I sometimes think I've missed something. Do you?
MARION. I don't know what you mean.
ESMERALDA. By always being at home. There's a certain—well, camaraderie in offices, I suppose. I'm very practical in my ways. I think I'd have made a success as a private secretary.
MARION. Yes, I'm sure you would.
ESMERALDA (*not looking at Marion*) Do you think I should have fallen in love with my employer?
MARION. In love . . .?
ESMERALDA. Yes.
MARION. Why do you ask me that?
ESMERALDA. I only know about these things from fiction in women's magazines. I gathered that it was almost inevitable, a sort of occupational hazard.
MARION. That's only in books.
ESMERALDA (*surprised*) You mean it doesn't happen in real life?
MARION. Not always. (*She moves towards the door* L) You must excuse me, Mrs Leigh.
ESMERALDA (*directly*) Are you in love with my husband?
MARION (*stopping and turning*) Are you joking?

ESMERALDA. No. Did it sound humorous?
MARION. I didn't think so.
ESMERALDA. Nor did I. It was a serious question.
MARION. I think you're taking advantage of my position here.
ESMERALDA. On the contrary. I wondered if *you* were.
MARION (*turning to the door*) Excuse me.
ESMERALDA. Please don't go. I'm not angry with you. I'd like to ask you one more question.
MARION (*turning*) What is it?
ESMERALDA. Is my husband in love with you?

(MARION *hesitates, then moves a step towards Esmeralda*)

MARION. Would you care?
ESMERALDA. Oh, no.
MARION (*crossing to* LC) Wouldn't you really!
ESMERALDA. Why should I?
MARION. You must have cared once.
ESMERALDA. Why?
MARION. You married him.
ESMERALDA. Yes, I did. I've spent the succeeding years wondering why. I suppose I must have seen something in him.
MARION. He must have seen something in you.
ESMERALDA (*smiling*) Yes, my bank account. (*She pauses briefly*) When your emotions are disturbed, Miss Dale, you cease to be the shrinking violet, don't you? You may take your spectacles off now if you wish. (*She pauses*) Yes, you are pretty. I think I wore spectacles when I met my husband. Rose-coloured ones. This is what marriage does to people who are ill-attuned to each other.
MARION (*crossing to* RC) You might have tried to be interested in his work. You could have helped him.
ESMERALDA. Did he tell you that? But of course he did. His wife doesn't understand him. That's the trouble. I do understand him. He has a very large capacity for writing weak melodramas and a very small capacity for earning a living.
MARION. It isn't true.
ESMERALDA. You do love him, don't you?
MARION. Yes, I do.
ESMERALDA. How odd of you! I warn you, you're going to be dreadfully disappointed.
MARION. I don't think so.
ESMERALDA. I don't suppose I thought so, either. Don't be deceived by his charm. There's nothing behind it. He's attractive, of course, but that's just the gilt on the—on the what? I assure you there's no gingerbread.
MARION. Perhaps you set too high a standard—for others.
ESMERALDA. Then be sure not to make the same mistake. Let your expectations be very low. He still won't come up to them.
MARION (*with an effort*) May I go now?

ESMERALDA (*casually*) Yes. (*She takes a magazine from the table* R *of the sofa, leans back and looks idly through the pages*)

(MARION *crosses towards the door* L, *then hesitates* LC)

(*She glances up*) Is there something on your mind?
MARION. Yes, there is.
ESMERALDA. Anything very important?
MARION. It's very important. (*She crosses to* RC) Mrs Leigh—may I ask you a question?
ESMERALDA. A favour?
MARION (*slowly*) I suppose it is.
ESMERALDA. Will you give me three guesses? You want me to divorce him. Is that it?
MARION. You don't love him.
ESMERALDA. I do not.
MARION. Then you don't want him.
ESMERALDA. I do not.
MARION. Then . . .
ESMERALDA (*rising*) Miss Dale, I'm not playing dog-in-the-manger. I'm sorry for you, just as I used to be sorry for myself when he had the power to disturb *my* peace of mind.
MARION. But you have no peace of mind. Living with a man you hate can give you nothing but misery.
ESMERALDA. I don't hate him. I despise him.
MARION (*leaning over the desk*) Then, for pity's sake, let him go.
ESMERALDA (*surprised*) Pity? For him or you?
MARION. If you've none for him, perhaps you might have for me.
ESMERALDA. I do pity you, Miss Dale. He's no good to you. You can't live on his charm. Luckily for us both I have money of my own. I take it that you are not so fortunate.
MARION. I've no money, if that's what you mean. I'm not ambitious. I'm used to being poor.
ESMERALDA. My husband isn't. His father kept him in luxury for twenty-five years and I took over from there. (*She crosses to the fireplace*)
MARION. You won't divorce him, Mrs Leigh?
ESMERALDA. You talk as if I'm the villain and you're the wronged woman. (*She moves to the sofa*) Aren't you confusing our respective roles?
MARION. If you were in love with him, and I'd come between you, then I'd be in the wrong. That isn't the case.

(*The cries of the gulls are heard*)

ESMERALDA (*moving to the window*) Miss Dale, I really can't discuss this any longer.
MARION (*moving to the upstage side of the window*) You won't divorce him.

ESMERALDA. Ten years ago Robert talked me out of a dozen better men who wanted to marry me. It didn't occur to me that anyone would marry me entirely for my money. Robert was the exception and I can't forgive him for it. Now he can pay for it.

MARION. I feel I must ask you just once more, Mrs Leigh?

ESMERALDA. You're very persistent.

MARION. I'm sorry. I must be. It's very important to me—and you.

ESMERALDA. My answer—sympathetically, Miss Dale—is still "No".

(MARION *crosses to the door* L)

Wait a minute . . . How important is it?

(MARION *opens the door and turns to face Esmeralda*)

MARION. It's a matter of life and death, Mrs Leigh.

(MARION *exits* L. *The sounds of a car arriving are heard off.* ESMERALDA *gazes thoughtfully after Marion for a moment, shrugs slightly and moves above the desk.*
TOM *appears in the doorway up* C *and whistles*)

ESMERALDA (*turning*) Come in, Tom.

TOM (*moving* C) You were looking very thoughtful.

ESMERALDA. Oh. I was just discussing a little matter with Miss Dale.

TOM. Miss Dale?

(*The cries of the gulls fade*)

ESMERALDA. My husband's secretary.

TOM. Oh, yes. She's pretty.

ESMERALDA. So you noticed it as well, did you?

TOM. As well?

ESMERALDA. I've noticed it, too.

TOM. If I could afford a secretary she's what I'd choose for myself. (*He signifies with his hands the outline of a feminine body. With a smile*) Do you know what I mean?

ESMERALDA (*smiling*) Would you like a drink before we go?

TOM. A quick one. Shall I get it myself?

ESMERALDA (*indicating the cupboard down* L) It's over there. Do you drink whisky?

TOM (*crossing to the cupboard down* L) I do drink whisky. (*He pours a whisky and soda for himself*) Will you have one?

ESMERALDA. A very small brandy.

TOM. Brandy for heroes, they say. What was the discussion between you and Miss Dale? (*He pours a brandy and soda for Esmeralda*)

ESMERALDA. Oh, it wasn't very important. My husband's new play. We were talking about the second act.

Tom. What about it?
Esmeralda. You wouldn't be interested.
Tom. Why not?
Esmeralda. Oh, well, there's a scene between two—two men. One of them is in love with the other's wife.
Tom. That's very original. So what?
Esmeralda. So he wants the husband to divorce her.
Tom (*picking up the drinks and crossing to Esmeralda*) This is even more original. And does he? (*He hands a drink to Esmeralda*)
Esmeralda. Agree to divorce her, you mean? No, he doesn't.
Tom. Why the heck should he if he still wants her for himself?

(MARION *enters* L. *She has a wrap around her shoulders*)

Marion (*moving* LC) I have rather a headache, Mrs Leigh, I'm going home.
Esmeralda. Yes, of course. (*She moves to the sofa and picks up her scarf and handbag*)
Tom. We're just off. Can we give you a lift?
Marion. No, thank you. I'd sooner walk.
Tom. Nonsense! Of course we'll give you a lift.
Esmeralda (*moving to* R *of the desk*) I was telling Mr Hammond about the scene in my husband's play.
Tom (*after a pause*) Do you think the husband ought to let his wife go if someone else wants her?
Marion. Under the circumstances.
Esmeralda. What circumstances?
Marion (*glancing at Esmeralda*) In Mr Leigh's play the husband is not in love with his wife. He loathes her. He doesn't want her for himself. He still won't let her go.
Tom. Why the hell not if he doesn't want her?
Esmeralda. Not everybody approves of divorce, you know. (*She hands her glass to Tom and moves up* C)

(MARION *moves up* C)

Are you ready?
Tom. Yes, sure. (*He puts his own and Esmeralda's glass on the window table*) What do they do? (*He moves to the door up* C)
Esmeralda. I don't know. It isn't finished yet. What can they do?
Tom. I only know what I'd do if I was the man and I wanted a woman badly enough. (*He turns to the door*)

(MARION *exits up* C)

Esmeralda. What would you do?
Tom (*turning to face Esmeralda*) I'd blow his brains out.

TOM *exits up* C. ESMERALDA *hesitates with her hand on the door knob as—*

the CURTAIN *falls*

Scene 3

SCENE—*The same. Two o'clock the following morning.*

When the CURTAIN *rises, the stage is in darkness. The window blind is closed, the room has been tidied and the table replaced down* R. ESMERALDA *unlocks the door up* C *and enters.* TOM *follows her on.* ESMERALDA *wears a coat. She switches on the lights.*

ESMERALDA. It's stifling. (*She glances at the clock*) It's two o'clock.
TOM. Isn't that dreadful!
ESMERALDA (*moving above the desk*) Thank you for bringing me home.
TOM (*closing the door*) Think nothing of it.
ESMERALDA. Did you like the barn dance?
TOM (*moving to* L *of Esmeralda*) Fine. I like this new-fangled square-dancing. I'm just old enough to remember the samba and the rumba. (*He dances* ESMERALDA *round*) You know, the old-fashioned leisurely stuff. (*He releases Esmeralda and moves* LC)

(ESMERALDA *removes her coat, puts it with her handbag on the desk chair and moves* C. *She gives the impression that she is waiting politely for Tom to go*)

ESMERALDA. It was nice of you to bring me home.
TOM. It wasn't nice of me at all. I never do anything unless I expect to get something out of it.
ESMERALDA (*coolly*) And what do you expect to get out of it?
TOM. I already got it. I got a kick out of bringing you home.
ESMERALDA (*thawing*) Oh! I see.
TOM (*sitting in the chair* LC *and facing her*) My eyes are tired. May I sit here and rest them on you?
ESMERALDA (*crossing to the cupboard down* L; *smiling*) I suppose you want a drink?
TOM (*pointing to the window table*) I was drinking whisky. I left my glass over there.
ESMERALDA. I'll give you a clean one.
TOM (*rising; crossing to the window table and picking up his glass*) Use the same one. We don't want too much crockery to wash up tomorrow morning. (*He crosses to Esmeralda and gives her the glass*)
ESMERALDA (*coolly*) Was that a joke? (*She pours a whisky and soda for Tom*)
TOM (*moving to the piano*) No, a dream. You fascinate me. I suppose you know that?
ESMERALDA. I didn't know.
TOM. Then it's time I told you. Wasn't it obvious?
ESMERALDA. Wasn't what obvious?
TOM. That I'm interested in you more than somewhat.
ESMERALDA (*moving to Tom and handing him the drink*) I thought it was Miss Dale who so closely approached your ideal.

Tom. As a secretary—and I'm not an idealist.
Esmeralda. You admire her.
Tom. Sure. I'd pick her out of a million for a secretary. She'd be fine to dictate to. Let me pay you a big compliment, Esmeralda. You're the one woman in a million I'd take dictation *from*.
Esmeralda (*crossing and sitting on the sofa*) I'm sure that's a very pretty compliment.
Tom. From me it's a very big one indeed. I don't take orders from many people.
Esmeralda. I believe you.
Tom (*perching himself on the left end of the desk*) It's a funny thing, I came back to England when I got out of the Army, because of an English woman. I was always told English women were reserved and cold. I never expected to have much time for them. I liked her, in a way. I like you in a bigger way. We'd get on together.
Esmeralda. What reason have you for thinking so?
Tom. We're different. That's why. Folks who are alike soon begin to bore each other. We'd never do that. I'll never settle anywhere very long—except with you if I get the chance. (*He pauses*) You and Robert don't get on. Why?
Esmeralda. We bore each other.
Tom. What are you doing about it?
Esmeralda. Nothing.
Tom. What's he doing?
Esmeralda (*looking directly at him*) What can he do?
Tom. Well, he can . . . (*He breaks off*)
Esmeralda. Yes?
Tom (*quickly*) I was going to say you could get a divorce. (*He goes on as if in the same sentence*) That's what you said his play was about, didn't you?
Esmeralda. Isn't it a coincidence!
Tom. Only you said two men and one woman. And this is . . .
Esmeralda. Two women and one man?
Tom. Who's the other woman?
Esmeralda (*smiling*) Who would it be?
Tom. So he is doing something about it after all. (*He puts his glass on the desk*)

(*There is a flash of lightning off*)

Hey! Summer lightning.
Esmeralda (*rising and crossing to* c) Tom, it's very late. You'd better go.
Tom (*rising and moving to* R *of Esmeralda*) Do you want me to go?
Esmeralda. Naturally. It's late.
Tom. Look, I'm not sixteen years old. My mother isn't waiting up for me.

ESMERALDA. Mine is. (*She turns from him*)
TOM. Let her wait. (*He swings her round, embraces her and fervently kisses her*)

(ESMERALDA *makes no response whatsoever.* TOM *releases her*)

ESMERALDA (*straightening her dress*) That wasn't very subtle, was it?

(TOM *picks up his glass, crosses to the cupboard down* L *and pours some whisky into the glass*)

TOM. It wasn't supposed to be subtle. (*He drains the glass and puts it on the radiogram*) I'm not subtle. I'm rough and clumsy. I did it because I wanted to. Because I had to. (*He moves up* C)
ESMERALDA. You don't have to apologize.
TOM. I never apologize. I told you I'm not a gentleman.
ESMERALDA (*laughing quite pleasantly*) All right. Tom, you're a hypocrite. You do your level best to sweep me off my feet and when it doesn't work you abuse me. Anyway, if you won't apologize to me, I will to you.
TOM. Why should you apologize? (*He moves to the door up* C)
ESMERALDA. I suppose I encouraged you.
TOM. I didn't notice if you did.
ESMERALDA. You mean you did that without encouragement? My, my! I tremble to think what would happen if I threw myself at your head.
TOM (*turning to the door*) So long!
ESMERALDA. Now you're sulking.
TOM (*turning*) I can stand anything from a woman except being laughed at.
ESMERALDA. Before you go, tell me one thing. Did you do that on the spur of the moment, because it seemed an easy thing to do, or does it go deeper?
TOM. Is that what froze you?
ESMERALDA. It contributed.
TOM. I see.
ESMERALDA. I'd hate to be made love to by a man who looked on me as a forgotten wife in need of a little random excitement.
TOM (*moving a step or two towards her*) I don't feel like that about you. Good God, you're not like that. If you had been—and I'd felt like that—do you suppose I'd still be here talking and feeling foolish?
ESMERALDA. I think in a peculiar sort of way, that was intended as a compliment.
TOM. It wasn't intended as a compliment. It was one. Good night, Esmeralda. (*He moves to the door up* C)
ESMERALDA (*moving to Tom*) Shall I see you again?
TOM. You don't want me to stay away?
ESMERALDA. By no means.

TOM. But don't expect me to have learned my lesson. I don't change, Esmeralda. Understand?
ESMERALDA. I understand perfectly.

TOM *exits up* C. ESMERALDA *stands in the doorway watching his departure. The sounds of a car departing are heard. There is a flash of lightning.* ESMERALDA *closes the door, locks it, then stands facing front for a moment and smiles slightly as if her thoughts were pleasurable. After a moment she yawns, not in boredom but in weariness, collects her coat and bag, switches off the lights, crosses to the cupboard down* L *and closes the doors. There is another flash of lightning.* ESMERALDA *crosses and exits* R. *After a moment, she re-enters, crosses to the piano, collects the box of cigarettes, then exits* R, *closing the door behind her. There is a flash of lightning, and a short silence broken by the creak of the door up* C *as it is cautiously opened.*

MARION *enters up* C, *moves to the desk, unlocks and opens the drawer and takes out the gun. There is a flash of lightning. After some hesitation,* MARION *crosses to the door* R, *opens it gently, exits and closes it quickly behind her. There is another flash of lightning. Three pistol shots are heard as—*

the CURTAIN *falls*

ACT II

Scene 1

Scene—*The same. Ten a.m. The same day*

When the Curtain *rises the room is empty and in darkness except for the gleams of pale September sunshine streaming through the blinds.* Gladys, *the occasional "help", enters* L. *She hums and whistles in turn a popular song of the day. The sound of a car arriving and stopping is heard off.* Gladys *crosses to the door up* c *and opens it. From time to time the wind and the surf are heard.* Gladys *crosses to the window, raises the blind, collects the dirty glass from the window table, moves to the fireplace, empties the ashtray from the mantelpiece into the glass, goes to the desk, empties the desk ashtray into the glass, picks up the dirty glasses from the desk and moves to the piano.*

Farrow (*off*) I suppose I ought to get back home, you know.

(Robert *enters up* c. *He carries a holdall*)

Robert (*as he enters*) You're a bachelor.

(Farrow *enters up* c)

You can go home any time. (*He moves to* R *of Gladys*) Good morning, Gladys.

Gladys. Good morning, sir. You're out early, aren't you?

Robert. On the contrary. I'm home late.

Gladys. Home late?

Robert. I stayed the night with Mr Farrow. (*He hands the holdall to Gladys*) Where is my wife?

Gladys. In bed, sir.

Robert. In bed?

Gladys. Yes. I've got a key. I let myself in.

Robert. You haven't seen Mrs Leigh?

Gladys. No, sir. I never disturb her.

Robert. Of course not. (*He turns to Farrow*) How about coffee?

Farrow (*moving to the sofa*) Good idea.

Robert. Gladys drinks coffee all day long. There's sure to be some ready. Is there, Gladys?

Gladys (*moving to the door* L) I'll just hot it up, sir.

(Farrow *sits on the sofa at the left end*)

Robert. Is my secretary here? (*He moves down* c)

Gladys. Not yet, sir.

(Gladys *exits* L)

ROBERT (*taking a cigarette from his case*) Marion wasn't too well yesterday. I've got an idea she won't be here today. (*He moves to the piano*)
FARROW. Esmeralda likes her bed, doesn't she?
ROBERT (*lighting his cigarette with the lighter on the piano*) It's only ten o'clock. She'd be at the local hop last night.
FARROW. Doesn't the girl take her morning tea?
ROBERT. Esmeralda has her little idiosyncrasies. She has an electric kettle. She makes tea about seven o'clock and then goes to sleep again. Well, I enjoyed the journey, Dick. (*He moves to the door up* C)
FARROW (*turning on the sofa to face Robert*) And the scene of the crime? Pretty grisly, wasn't it?
ROBERT. Fascinating. Horrible, but strangely fascinating. (*He moves down* C) It's curious how an ordinary little house—suddenly begins to look evil because something evil happened in it. Or would it always look evil? (*He circles the table* LC *and moves to the desk*)
FARROW. It's the association of ideas. Whenever I think of Calcutta I think of the Black Hole of Calcutta. Now this lonely farmhouse we've visited can never mean anything to us except a girl who was done to death.
ROBERT (*perching himself on the left end of the desk*) Do you think the boy did it?
FARROW. I wouldn't know. I just remembered something, Robert. Immediately I've swallowed the coffee I'd better be on my way. I have to telephone London.
ROBERT (*rising and taking a couple of steps towards the telephone*) Use my phone.
FARROW. Can't. I have to check up on some documents before I make the call.

(ROBERT *moves up* C)

(*Thoughtfully*) The pillow was absolutely saturated with blood.
ROBERT (*turning to face Farrow; aghast*) What—did you say?
FARROW (*surprised*) The pillow.
ROBERT. What about the pillow? You say it's . . .
FARROW. It was absolutely saturated with blood.
ROBERT. Oh, you mean where the girl was murdered. Stupid of me. I hate the mention of such things. (*He moves to the desk chair and sits*)

(FARROW *looks intently at Robert*)

I'm sorry. Actually the experience was out of my line. I greatly appreciate your taking me. It was grand of you. But it was too much for me.
FARROW. I hadn't realized.

ROBERT. Yes. I was quite sick. I thought I'd faint and make a fool of myself. Not very manly, eh?

FARROW. I wouldn't say that. I'm used to it. You wouldn't have been the first man to faint.

ROBERT. It's nice of you to say so.

FARROW. No, it's true. I've seen a fourteen-stone policeman as tough as hickory who couldn't stand the sight of blood. I should have had more sense. You seemed all right at the time.

ROBERT. I assure you—not without considerable effort.

(GLADYS *enters* L. *She carries a tray with two cups of coffee and a basin of sugar*)

GLADYS (*crossing above the desk to* R *of it*) Coffee, sir. (*She puts the tray on the desk. To Farrow*) Help yourself to the sugar, sir.

FARROW (*rising*) Thank you, Gladys. (*He takes a cup of coffee and sugars it*)

GLADYS (*to Robert*) Sugar, sir?

ROBERT (*preoccupied*) No.

(GLADYS *crosses and exits* L)

I suppose the farm labourer killed her. He's a shifty-looking character. I didn't like the look of him.

FARROW (*facing front*) Don't judge people by their faces, Robert.

ROBERT. But those eyes—the furtive way they avoided you—I wouldn't trust him a yard. Would you?

FARROW. He wasn't pretty. (*He sips his coffee*)

ROBERT. He certainly wasn't.

FARROW. But you can't put a chap in the dock because he's ugly.

ROBERT. No.

FARROW. Then there is the question of motive. Love, jealousy, greed, sudden violence—and so on. (*He sips his coffee*)

ROBERT. But if there's no motive at all, that makes it extremely difficult, doesn't it?

FARROW. There's always a motive. Unless, of course, it's a psychopathic killer who goes round committing murder for the sheer love of it. (*He sips his coffee*)

ROBERT. And he's a madman.

(FARROW *finishes his coffee*)

FARROW. Yes. (*He puts his cup on the tray*) Thank you for the coffee. I really must go.

ROBERT (*rising*) Of course. (*He crosses to* LC *and calls*) Gladys. (*To Farrow*) Esmeralda would be furious if I let you go without her seeing you. (*He stubs out his cigarette*)

FARROW. Please don't disturb her.

(GLADYS *enters* L)

ROBERT (*taking a cigarette from his case*) It's time she put in an appearance. (*To Gladys*) Gladys, see if Mrs Leigh is awake, will you?

(GLADYS *crosses to the door* R)

FARROW. Really, Robert!
ROBERT (*to Gladys*) Tell her Mr Farrow is just leaving.
GLADYS. Yes, sir.

(GLADYS *exits* R, *leaving the door open.* ROBERT *crosses to* L, *faces* R *and observes closely.* FARROW, *at ease, is more relaxed*)

FARROW. I shall blame you for waking her. (*He pauses*) She was probably very late to bed.

(ROBERT *lights his cigarette.* GLADYS, *off* R, *screams.* ROBERT, *expecting such a thing, stares with simulated surprise at Farrow. The sound of the surf is heard*)

What on earth . . .? (*He moves to the door* R)

(GLADYS *enters* R)

(*To Gladys*) What happened? Is something wrong?
GLADYS. Only me, sir. I saw a snake.
ROBERT. A snake?

(FARROW *laughs*)

GLADYS. Yes, sir. On the verandah. It made me jump. (*She crosses below the desk to* R *of Robert*) You needn't look so worried, sir. I'm all right now. (*To Farrow*) It was a long brown one.
FARROW. A grass snake, perhaps. Or an adder.
ROBERT. But—didn't you see Mrs Leigh?
GLADYS. There now, I clean forgot. It sent everything else out of my head. (*Casually*) Mrs Leigh isn't there.
ROBERT (*crossing below Gladys to the door* R) She—isn't there?
GLADYS. No, sir. (*She moves below the piano*)
ROBERT. But she should be there. (*He turns and gazes at the door* R)

(ESMERALDA, *unseen by the others, appears at the door up* C. *She is very cool and faintly smiling, and carries some roses she has cut from the garden*)

ESMERALDA. Good morning, gentlemen.

(FARROW *and* ROBERT *turn.* ROBERT *stares at Esmeralda*)

FARROW. Morning, my dear.
ESMERALDA. Good morning, Gladys.
GLADYS. Good morning, ma'am.

(GLADYS *exits* L. ROBERT *continues to stare at Esmeralda*)

ESMERALDA (*to Robert*) Is something wrong? (*She moves to the desk*)
ROBERT. You weren't in your room.
ESMERALDA. Should I be?
ROBERT. But I . . .
ESMERALDA. Yes, Robert?
ROBERT (*moving to the fireplace*) Nothing. I . . . Nothing.
ESMERALDA (*putting the roses on the desk*) You look as if you've seen a ghost. Or as if you expected to see one. What time did you get back?
FARROW. Two o'clock. (*He crosses down* LC) I'm afraid Robert had a poor night. He was up for hours in his room.
ROBERT. How do you know that?
FARROW. I'm a policeman. I counted the cigarette stubs in your ashtray.
ESMERALDA. You're very observant, Dick. (*To Robert*) Smoking in bed is a dangerous habit.
FARROW. He wasn't in bed.
ESMERALDA. Wasn't he?
FARROW (*with a step to* C) He was walking up and down half the night. Every so often he would sit down, smoke a cigarette, and then get up and go over to the window and crush it out.
ROBERT (*very surprised*) Were you in the room with me? Or is there a hole in the wall?
FARROW. Nothing so obvious. A wicker chair. Every time you got into it or out of it, it creaked. There were stubs in the ashtray by the window and the one beside the chair.
ESMERALDA. Q.E.D. (*To Robert*) Had you something on your mind, Robert? Couldn't you sleep?
ROBERT (*stubbing out his cigarette in the ashtray on the mantelpiece*) I dozed off—I think—in fits and starts.
FARROW. Did you hear me go out at six o'clock?
ROBERT (*more surprised*) Go out? Did you go out?
FARROW. Yes.
ROBERT. Why did you go out?
FARROW. Inspector Lewis phoned me at six. Didn't you hear him? I suppose you had dropped off by then. Something very exciting cropped up in a case he's dealing with, and he asked me to go round to see him.
ROBERT. You mean you weren't in the house all the time?
FARROW. No.

(ROBERT *laughs and looks front*)

Why?
ROBERT. Oh, no reason.
ESMERALDA. Does it matter, Robert, that he wasn't in the house all the time?
ROBERT. No. Not at all.

ESMERALDA. It seemed to upset you. (*To Farrow*) I suppose it's being on the scene of the crime. It must be quite nerve-racking.
ROBERT (*turning to face Esmeralda; tensely*) Scene of the crime?
ESMERALDA. That's why you went to Somerset, isn't it?
ROBERT. Oh, yes. (*He pauses briefly*) My brain simply wouldn't relax.
ESMERALDA. It was pretty late when I went to bed. Tom Hammond brought me back from the village hall. Wasn't it nice of him?
ROBERT. What time was that?
ESMERALDA. Two o'clock. Why do you ask?
ROBERT. No reason.
ESMERALDA. I went to my room as soon as he left, but I didn't go straight to bed.
ROBERT. Why not? Why didn't you?
ESMERALDA. It was such a stifling night. Did you see the sky? I stood awhile on the verandah and it seemed I could almost reach out my hand to touch the sky.
FARROW. We didn't spend a peaceful night.
ESMERALDA. Oh, neither did I. I didn't get any sleep at all. My rest was disturbed.
ROBERT. Why?
ESMERALDA (*as if preoccupied*) What did you say?
ROBERT. You said your rest was disturbed.
ESMERALDA. The magpies.

(FARROW *laughs*)

(*To Farrow*) They're noisy beasts, aren't they? I got dressed early for once. That's the one reward of a sleepless night. You see the dawn. It was particularly beautiful and it made me feel glad to be alive. (*She indicates the roses*) I cut these whilst the dew was on them. (*She selects a bud and moves to Farrow*)

(ROBERT *moves to the window*).

You're fond of roses, Dick, aren't you? May I?
FARROW. Exquisite, aren't they?
ESMERALDA (*putting the bud in Farrow's lapel*) This one's called Zephyrine Droughin. Isn't that a wonderful name? (*To Robert*) Isn't Miss Dale coming to work today? (*She moves to the piano*)
ROBERT. I don't know.
ESMERALDA (*moving to the desk*) Surely you do.
ROBERT (*moving to the fireplace; disturbed*) No.
ESMERALDA. You are her employer, aren't you?
ROBERT. She wasn't well yesterday.
ESMERALDA. I didn't hear her complain.
ROBERT. Nevertheless, she did. A headache.
ESMERALDA. She isn't coming, then?
ROBERT (*facing Esmeralda*) I don't know, I tell you.

ESMERALDA. There's no need to get excited about it. (*She picks up the roses and crosses to Farrow*) I merely want to know how many to expect to lunch. Can you stay, Dick?
FARROW (*moving to the door up* C) Thank you, but not another moment. I really must be off.
ESMERALDA (*moving to the door* L) Steak and onions.
FARROW. I'd like that enormously. (*He smiles*) I must still leave you.
ESMERALDA (*putting the roses on the piano and crossing to Farrow*) I'll see you off. (*She takes his arm. To Robert*) Did you profit from your excursion into the realms of violence? (*She looks straight at Robert*) Was the experience useful?
ROBERT. I think it might be.
ESMERALDA (*to Farrow*) Did it upset his stomach?
FARROW. I'm afraid it did.
ESMERALDA (*looking at Robert*) He has a weak one, you know. I can't imagine why anyone so squeamish should play about with murder.
FARROW. Play about with it?
ESMERALDA. Write a play about it. It's violence at secondhand, isn't it? The author works out the details and he selects a suitable character to go through the actual performance. It's cowardly, in a way.
FARROW (*laughing*) I wouldn't call it that.
ESMERALDA. I would.
FARROW. You're rather harsh on authors, aren't you?
ESMERALDA. It depends what they're the authors of, doesn't it?
FARROW. I'm going. This is over my head. See you later, Bob.
ROBERT (*moving to the door up* C) Yes. Thank you, Dick, for taking me along.

(ESMERALDA *and* FARROW *exit up* C. ROBERT *stands watching them off. The sounds of a car starting and departing are heard*)

(*He crosses to the door* R, *opens it, looks off for a moment, closes the door, crosses to the desk, looks in the desk drawer, closes it, then moves* C *and calls*) Gladys.

(GLADYS *enters* L)

Gladys, I suppose you haven't seen Miss Dale?
GLADYS. No, sir.
ROBERT. Was my wife out when you got here?
GLADYS. I don't know. I thought she was in bed.
ROBERT. Was the door locked?
GLADYS. Yes. I've got a key.
ROBERT. I know you have. You left the door open?
GLADYS. To let the fresh air in.
ROBERT. No doubt Mrs Leigh went out whilst you were in the kitchen.

GLADYS. Is something wrong, sir?
ROBERT. I don't suppose so.

(*The telephone rings*)

(*He crosses to the telephone and lifts the receiver. Into the telephone*) Hello . . . Marion . . . Miss Dale? . . . (*He stands with his back to the door up* C)

(GLADYS *exits* L)

Oh, yes, you're Marion's aunt. Is she all right? . . .

(ESMERALDA, *unseen by Robert, enters up* C *and stands in silence by the door, a very faint smile about her mouth. The sound of the surf fades*)

(*He becomes agitated*) I'm glad you called. I was anxious . . . No, she isn't here . . . You mean, you didn't see her this morning? . . . Are you sure? . . . Yes, of course, you couldn't be mistaken about such a thing . . . What—where do you imagine she is? . . . She went to bed. You're sure of that? . . . She wasn't there when you got up at nine o'clock . . . No, I don't know anything. I was away all night, so I couldn't know . . . Her bed was slept in, wasn't it? . . . I don't understand at all . . .
ESMERALDA. Ask if her bedroom window was open.

(ROBERT *turns and faces Esmeralda*)

ROBERT (*into the telephone*) I'll come immediately. We may have to inform the police . . . And, of course, there may be a very simple explanation. (*He replaces the receiver*)
ESMERALDA (*moving to the desk*) It may have the simplest explanation in the world.
ROBERT. What do you know about it?
ESMERALDA. Is something wrong?
ROBERT. That was Marion's aunt, as I imagine you heard. She's worried about her.
ESMERALDA. Can't she find her?
ROBERT. Do you know where she is?
ESMERALDA. What a ridiculous question. Should I?
ROBERT. Why did you say: "Ask if her bedroom window was open?"
ESMERALDA. Just a hunch. Young girls living with maiden aunts are driven to the most desperate measures. You've no idea. (*She leans on the left end of the desk*) Perhaps she has a lover. You're taking it very much to heart. After all, she's only your secretary. You're as anxious about her as you would be about me. Why were you so surprised to see me when I came in?
ROBERT. I wasn't surprised.
ESMERALDA. Really?

ROBERT (*taking a cigarette from his case*) We thought you were in your room. That's all.

ESMERALDA. Is that where you expected to find me?

ROBERT (*pausing in the act of lighting his cigarette*) Why should I?

ESMERALDA. But you should. I often stay in bed until late.

ROBERT (*crossing to the window*) Oh, yes. If that's what you mean.

ESMERALDA. What else could I mean?

(*They face each other in silence for a few moments*)

ROBERT (*moving a step down* R; *as if casually*) How long did Hammond stay?

ESMERALDA. He didn't stay.

ROBERT. He brought you here at two o'clock.

ESMERALDA. Yes.

ROBERT (*moving up* C) What time did he leave?

ESMERALDA. Shortly afterwards.

ROBERT (*quickly*) How shortly?

ESMERALDA (*moving* LC *and facing Robert*) Are you playing the jealous husband?

ROBERT (*moving level with her*) Not in the least.

ESMERALDA. Then I don't understand. You're asking the most unusual questions, you know. I don't believe for one moment you're jealous of Tom Hammond. Whatever my faults—and you find so many—I usually speak the truth. He brought me here—I gave him a drink—and then he went away.

ROBERT. It must have been a severe disappointment for him.

ESMERALDA. I believe it was. Are there any more enquiries you wish to make?

ROBERT (*moving to the door up* C) I am going to see Marion's aunt. If Marion's missing we'll have to report it to the police.

ESMERALDA. Surely that's a job for her aunt. After all, she's only an employee. Or is she?

ROBERT (*deciding not to reply to the last question*) Let's hope she's already turned up by the time I get there.

ESMERALDA. Don't be *too* disappointed if she hasn't.

(ROBERT *is again on the point of speaking, decides not to and exits up* C. ESMERALDA *moves to the door up* C *and looks after Robert. Her expression changes from smiling mockery to grim determination. She moves to the window.*

GLADYS *enters* L)

GLADYS (*crossing to the desk*) Can I collect the coffee-cups, ma'am?

ESMERALDA (*moving to the fireplace*) Yes. (*She takes a cigarette from the box on the mantelpiece, and lights it*)

GLADYS. Thank you. (*She picks up the coffee tray*) Shall I dust your bedroom or do you want to do it yourself?

ESMERALDA (*moving to the window*) I'll do it.

(GLADYS *crosses to the door* L)

(*She appears to see someone through the window and turns to Gladys*) Leave the coffee-cups in the kitchen, Gladys. You may go home now.

GLADYS (*stopping and turning*) Go home?

ESMERALDA. Yes. I shall pay you your full wages, of course.

GLADYS. You mean you don't even want me to wash and dry them? Go home straight away?

ESMERALDA. Please. I can't explain why.

GLADYS. If you say so, ma'am. I'll put 'em at the side of the sink. (*Puzzled, but not displeased, she turns to the door, hesitates, turns and moves* LC)

(*The cries of the gulls are heard*)

When you see the dirty pots, ma'am, I hope you'll remember you told me to leave 'em.

ESMERALDA. Don't worry about that.

GLADYS. Good morning, ma'am.

ESMERALDA. Good morning, Gladys.

(GLADYS *exits* L. ESMERALDA *sits on the window seat.* TOM *is seen to pass the window from* R *to* L. *He wears a jersey and yachting cap.* ESMERALDA *rises and moves to the door up* C.

TOM *enters up* C)

Tom.

TOM. Are you alone? (*He puts his cap on the window table*)

ESMERALDA. Yes, Robert's out. I got rid of the maid. Is it all right?

TOM. I don't know.

ESMERALDA. You don't know—did anyone see you?

TOM. Nobody saw me go.

ESMERALDA. They saw you come back.

TOM. Sure, with fish in the bottom of the boat. I trawled for a couple of hours. It was good camouflage. (*He crosses to the door* R. *Anxiously*) What about your room? Did you make a thorough examination?

ESMERALDA. Yes.

TOM (*opening the door* R *and looking off*) Would anyone know she's been there?

(*The cries of the gulls fade*)

ESMERALDA. No.

TOM (*turning to face her*) You checked and double checked. They couldn't tell not even with a microscope and all the rest of the gadgets they use. Is that right? (*He closes the door*)

ESMERALDA. Yes, that's right.

TOM. Good. (*He moves to* R *of Esmeralda*)

ESMERALDA. There was only—the rug.

TOM (*crossing to the cupboard down* L) That's at the bottom of the sea.

ESMERALDA. And the gun?

TOM. That's there too. Did we miss anything? (*He pours a drink for himself*)

ESMERALDA. No—(*she closes the door up* C) everything's all right.

TOM. I hope to hell it is. I'm in this up to the neck. (*He moves* LC) When you phoned me, how did you know I'd come?

ESMERALDA (*moving* C) I didn't know. I thought you might.

TOM (*moving to* L *of her*) Well, you were right. I come round here in the middle of the night and there's a dead body and you want me to dump it in the sea. So I do. A mile out, so that she'll never come back again. But I don't understand everything.

ESMERALDA. I told you plainly enough.

TOM (*crossing below Esmeralda to the desk*) I know you did—but I wasn't perfectly relaxed. (*He sits on the left end of the desk and faces Esmeralda*) I couldn't think straight. Maybe it was the girl's body that took the edge off my concentration.

ESMERALDA. Please! You don't know how awful it was. I went to my room and I went on the verandah. It was a stifling night and I stood there watching the sky. Suddenly I heard a sound in the garden. You had just gone and I was alone. I keep a revolver in my room. I got it out of the drawer and went back on to the verandah. Then I heard someone moving softly in the house, so I waited. I was terrified. Then very quietly my door opened and Marion came in. I watched her from behind the curtain. She couldn't understand why I wasn't in bed. Then she looked up. She was so surprised when she saw me that the gun fell out of her hand. I didn't give her time to pick it up.

TOM. Then you let her have it? (*He drains his glass and puts it on the desk*)

ESMERALDA. Yes, I did. I fired three times. I made certain. I really did make certain.

TOM (*rising and moving to the fireplace*) You sure did.

ESMERALDA (*moving to the desk*) It was self-defence. She tried to kill me.

TOM (*with a step or two towards the sofa*) Maybe we weren't very clever after all. She came here to kill you. Since when is self-defence a crime? You could have come out in the open and got away with it.

ESMERALDA. I didn't want it to be like that.

TOM. What do you mean?

ESMERALDA. As you say, I could have got away with it on grounds of self-defence, but that wouldn't have involved Robert. He would have got off scot-free. That isn't what I intend him to do.

TOM. What are you getting at?

Esmeralda. Robert wanted to kill me. He hadn't the courage to do it himself, so he got Marion to make the attempt. (*She moves to* L *of the door up* C) I'm going to make him pay for it.

Tom (*moving to* R *of the door up* C) Now just a minute. Are you sure he was involved in it?

Esmeralda. Quite sure. She was his mistress.

Tom. How do you know?

Esmeralda. I talked to her. She wanted me to divorce him. She said it was of the greatest importance to her. Then she said: "It's a matter of life and death." Naturally I didn't understand at the time. But I do now.

Tom (*crossing and sitting on the piano stool*) If I was sure he'd been behind her . . . But there's no proof. We don't know, Esmeralda.

Esmeralda. I know.

Tom. You think so. You're pretty certain. You don't really know.

Esmeralda. Suppose I did have proof. What would you do?

Tom. Have you?

Esmeralda. Yes. He had a perfect alibi. He was away with Dick Farrow who's a V.I.P. at Scotland Yard.

Tom. That's not proof.

Esmeralda. Listen, there is a diamond bracelet missing from my room. Robert must have taken it with him yesterday when he came back here expecting to find me dead. He could have said the thief took the bracelet and killed me. You should have seen him when he walked in with Farrow. After some casual conversation he became anxious about me. He wondered if something was wrong. And then more casual conversation to pave the way to his finally discovering me. He hadn't even the guts to do it himself. He sent Gladys.

Tom. He's a louse. He's got a genius for letting women do his dirty work for him.

Esmeralda. Yes, hasn't he. He was so shocked when he knew I wasn't in my room. You should have seen his face when I walked in at the front door. He thought I was dead all right. Now do you know how I feel?

Tom (*rising and moving down* C) The dirty bastard. My God, I'll make him pay for this. I'll hit him so hard you won't be able to recognize him. I'll beat him up . . .

Esmeralda. I want more than that.

Tom (*turning to face her; quickly*) What are you driving at?

Esmeralda (*moving to* L *of Tom*) I'll tell you exactly what I'm driving at. I don't want someone to start a little fight with him and send him home with a few bruises and a little spilled blood. I want more, I tell you.

(Tom *stares more soberly at Esmeralda*)

TOM. How much more? (*He takes hold of her*) How much more, Esmeralda? (*He backs away a few paces*) My God, I thought I was the tough one. I believe you're tougher than I am.

ESMERALDA. But you're stronger. That's why I need your help.

TOM (*sitting on the sofa at the left end*) But—murder!

ESMERALDA. It isn't murder. It's revenge.

TOM. What's the difference?

ESMERALDA (*crossing and sitting R of Tom on the sofa*) Do you remember what you told me at the dance last night—but perhaps you didn't mean it?

TOM. I said you were beautiful.

ESMERALDA. Yes.

TOM. I also said you were the sort of woman I'd commit any crime on the calendar to possess.

ESMERALDA. Yes.

TOM. I remember. (*He rises and crosses to the fireplace*) Which are you interested in—(*he turns to face her*) me or revenge?

ESMERALDA. Both.

TOM. It's got to be both. I told you if I do anything I expect to get something out of it. (*He moves to her*) I name my own price.

ESMERALDA. What is it?

TOM. You.

ESMERALDA. I'm willing to pay.

TOM. Not just willing. That won't do.

ESMERALDA. Good God! Why do you think I let you bring me home last night? I didn't need any help then. Why do you suppose Robert's jealous of you? Yes, jealous—even if he doesn't want me for himself. When I needed help last night, why do you suppose you were the first person I turned to?

TOM. You tell me.

ESMERALDA. You want it in words?

TOM. Yes, I want it in words.

ESMERALDA. Am I the first woman who's found you attractive?

TOM (*pulling Esmeralda to her feet*) Would you go away with me? Do I mean so much to you?

ESMERALDA. Do I—to you?

TOM. You're the only woman I've ever known who did. (*He takes her roughly in his arms and kisses her*)

ESMERALDA. Tom—(*she gazes admiringly at him*) you'll never realize how much I've wanted a man like you. He wanted to get rid of me, didn't he? Well, now I want to get rid of him. (*She kisses Tom briefly, but passionately*) Tom, I *can* trust you, can't I?

TOM. Every inch of the way.

ESMERALDA. I know I can. Yes, I know it. (*She breaks from him and moves to the piano*) I'll play him at his own game, that's what I'll do.

TOM (*crossing to her*) How?

ESMERALDA. Give me time. It can be done. I'll find a way.

TOM. Well, it had better be good—the way we go about it. I'm conceited about one thing—my neck. I like it.
ESMERALDA. So do I. Your head sits prettily on it.
TOM (*collecting his glass from the desk; as if in one sentence*) It's going to stay that way. (*He crosses to the cupboard down* L) Let's drink to the new partnership. (*He pours two whiskies and hands one to Esmeralda*)

(ESMERALDA *sniffs at her glass and pulls a wry face*)

This is a unique occasion.
ESMERALDA (*raising her glass*) To us. May we succeed where others failed.

They drink as—

the CURTAIN *falls*

SCENE 2

SCENE—*The same. Two days later. Early afternoon.*

When the CURTAIN *rises,* ESMERALDA *is standing at the window, smoking, with her back to the audience.* ROBERT *enters up* C. *He halts as he sees Esmeralda. They look at each other and it is he who glances away.*

ROBERT. Dick Farrow's on his way here. (*He closes the door up* C) He wants a word with you.
ESMERALDA (*turning*) Oh?
ROBERT. About Marion.
ESMERALDA (*moving to* R *of the sofa*) Does he think I can help him to find her?
ROBERT. I don't know what he thinks.
ESMERALDA. Do *you* think so, Robert?
ROBERT (*moving above the desk chair*) Why should I?
ESMERALDA. You shouldn't. Tom Hammond took her home. There was no reason for her to come back here. Was there, Robert?
ROBERT. What did happen, Esmeralda?

(ESMERALDA *is quite shocked*)

She did come here, didn't she? You did see her?
ESMERALDA (*moving below the sofa*) How can you possibly know that, Robert. You were miles away in Somerset with Mr Farrow of Scotland Yard. Mr Farrow would testify that you were away all night. You couldn't possibly know that Marion came back here.
ROBERT. You know she did.
ESMERALDA. Do I, Robert? If you know anything about Marion's activities, I think you should tell Dick Farrow.

ROBERT (*moving a little down* C) You're extremely clever, Esmeralda.

ESMERALDA. And you, Robert, are not.

ROBERT (*after a pause*) Who helped you? Somebody helped you.

ESMERALDA. If you're accusing me of something you must clarify the charge. You're in rather a spot, aren't you? If you push *me* over, you fall, don't you?

ROBERT (*with a step towards her*) Yes, *you* know. You know all right.

ESMERALDA (*moving to the fireplace*) Do I, Robert? (*She stubs out her cigarette in the ashtray on the mantelpiece*)

ROBERT (*crossing to Esmeralda and turning her to face him*) What did you do?

ESMERALDA. I went quietly to bed as a good wife should. What did you do? Shall we both tell Dick Farrow what we did? I dare if you dare.

ROBERT (*backing a pace from her*) You—you hypocrite! I hope you're very proud of your achievement.

ESMERALDA. I haven't achieved anything. You made an attempt. I didn't. I don't consider I've won anything. But you lost, Robert.

ROBERT. Yes. Then you admit it?

ESMERALDA. No. No, Robert. I admit nothing.

ROBERT. I ought to kill you.

ESMERALDA. But you won't. You'd have to do it yourself.

(ROBERT *slaps Esmeralda's face*)

Really, Robert! (*She laughs at him*)

ROBERT (*crossing to* LC) Now what do we do?

(*The sounds of a car arriving and stopping are heard*)

ESMERALDA. What can we do?

ROBERT (*moving to the piano*) I don't know. Certainly we can't continue to live together. Every moment would be hell.

ESMERALDA. I agree.

ROBERT. Every time I looked at you I'd think of—of her, and I'd hate you for it.

(*The cries of the gulls are heard*)

ESMERALDA. And *I'd* think of her, and despise and hate *you* for it.

ROBERT (*turning to her*) I suppose you still won't agree to a divorce?

ESMERALDA. It won't be necessary. (*She suddenly motions Robert to be silent*)

(FARROW *appears at the door up* C)

ROBERT. Dick, I didn't know you were here.
FARROW (*coming into the room*) I just got here.
ESMERALDA (*sitting on the sofa*) Hello, Dick.
FARROW (*moving down* C) This is a most unhappy affair, isn't it?

(ROBERT *lights a cigarette for himself*)

ESMERALDA. Is there still no trace of her?
FARROW (*to Robert*) She just vanished off the face of the earth. The police seem to be helpless. Of course, I've really no connexion with the case. (*He sits in the desk chair*) But as I know all the people concerned in it, I want to help where I can.
ESMERALDA (*shrewdly*) Why do you say—"all the people concerned in the case"? Are there any?
FARROW (*apologetically*) I mean I know you and Robert, and I knew Miss Dale herself. I didn't say "concerned in her disappearance". Did you think I did?
ESMERALDA. I had to be sure.

(*The cries of the gulls fade*)

FARROW (*to Esmeralda*) I know you've already discussed it with the police, but I want you to think very hard and see if you can dig something up that would help. Did she confide in you, Esmeralda?
ESMERALDA. Really, I knew her very slightly. Robert knew her more intimately than I.
FARROW. Yes. I wondered if she was having an unhappy love affair or something like that.
ESMERALDA. I got the impression that there was a man.
FARROW. Did she tell you so?
ESMERALDA. I couldn't say.
FARROW. But, surely . . .
ESMERALDA. No, I don't think she did. It was just an impression I had. Perhaps I was wrong.
FARROW. She left here in the early afternoon, you said.
ESMERALDA (*nodding*) Yes.
FARROW. And she didn't come back?
ESMERALDA. There was no reason why she should.
FARROW. No. Can we say you're quite certain that she didn't come back?
ESMERALDA. Oh, no. She might have. But I can't think of a reason why she should. Can you, Robert?
ROBERT (*moving up* C) No.
FARROW. Tom Hammond, I understand, called here for you with his car. Miss Dale went with you both as far as the bungalow she shared with her aunt.

(ROBERT *moves to the window*)

ESMERALDA. Yes.
FARROW. Then you and Hammond went for a sail.
ESMERALDA. Yes.
FARROW. And that night he brought you home after the dance?
ESMERALDA. He came in for a drink and then he left. I told you so. It was all extremely dignified.

(TOM *appears at the door up* C)

FARROW. Did you know that he went out all night in his boat?
ESMERALDA. I heard so. He's rather crazy, isn't he? Canadians don't live by the clock as we do.
TOM (*coming into the room; quite confidently*) Was there any harm in it? (*To Esmeralda and Robert*) I was passing by. (*He moves down* C *and faces Farrow*) Did I do wrong?
FARROW. Did I give that impression? Certainly not. Only, you see, I have to know every detail about this affair. There's a man in the case somewhere . . .
TOM. Well, don't look at me.
FARROW. I have to look at everybody. Don't worry, Hammond. I'm only asking questions. You took your boat out that night.
TOM. I often do.
FARROW. It was tied up at the far end of the beach, wasn't it?
TOM. It may have been. I don't remember.
FARROW. It was. I've made sure of the fact.
TOM. I'm not denying it. So what?

(FARROW *takes Marion's wrist-watch from his pocket and holds it out*)

FARROW. Have you seen this before?

(ROBERT *moves to* R *of Farrow and takes the watch from him*)

ROBERT. It's Marion's watch. Where did you find it?
FARROW (*taking the watch from Robert*) On the beach.
TOM. I never saw it before. (*Angrily*) What's it got to do with me? Young Haslemere and his wife were out all night. So were a couple of the fishing boats.
FARROW. You're getting excited.
TOM. Sure I am. I only spoke to the woman a couple of times. Ask Haslemere about it. Ask the people in the fishing boat.
FARROW (*quietly*) I already have.
TOM. Well?
FARROW. They didn't see Miss Dale near the beach.
TOM. Neither did I.
FARROW. Thank you. That's all I was going to ask you.
TOM (*moving below the piano; grunting*) Oh!

FARROW. It looks like suicide, doesn't it?
ROBERT. She wouldn't kill herself. I knew her better than that.
ESMERALDA. Can you think of a better explanation?
ROBERT (*after a slight hesitation*) No. (*He moves to the window*) No, I don't suppose so.
TOM (*to Farrow*) Do you think she committed suicide?
FARROW. I don't know. If you're asking my opinion I'd say no. As a matter of fact I'm not even convinced that she's dead.
ROBERT (*turning*) Of course she's dead!
FARROW. Oh!
ROBERT (*alarmed*) I mean, she must be.
FARROW. Why?
ROBERT (*bewildered*) Why?
FARROW. We haven't found her body.
ROBERT. If she was alive, would she have disappeared?
FARROW. You wouldn't suppose so. But people do.
ROBERT. Why should she?
FARROW. Ah, that's a direct question. The Inspector Lewis has a theory about it.
TOM. Oh, what sort of a theory?
FARROW. He thinks there's a man in the case. He thinks it's possible she went off with him.
TOM. What about the watch?
FARROW. We only found it today. One of the people in the village, a local inhabitant, is almost willing to swear he saw her on the beach at dawn.
ROBERT (*moving to* R *of the desk*) That's impossible!

(*The others look at Robert*)

ESMERALDA. It's possible, Robert.
ROBERT (*bitterly*) Yes, it's possible.
FARROW. Robert, the night she disappeared you and I were away.
ROBERT. Yes.
FARROW. We got back—to the station, that is—at two o'clock in the morning. We slept at my house, which is only fifty yards from the beach.
ROBERT. Yes.
FARROW. Did you leave the house at all whilst I was out between six and seven-thirty?
ROBERT. No, I did not.
FARROW. You didn't go as far as the beach?
ROBERT. No. Why do you ask?
FARROW. I wondered if you'd seen anything that might help us. If Miss Dale's watch was found on the beach—as in fact it was—presumably she must have been there.
ROBERT. But if I knew anything, man, I should have said so long before this. You don't suppose . . .

FARROW. I'm sorry. (*He rises*) The idea just occurred to me. (*He moves to the door up* C *and turns to face Robert*) We don't seem to get much further, do we?
ROBERT (*moving to* R *of Farrow; intently*) Just a moment. You can't ask me questions like that and then casually say you're sorry. Why did you ask me?
FARROW. Often the most important evidence comes out in the least expected manner—perhaps a detail that's been overlooked. I assure you, that's the only reason I asked.
ROBERT (*turning to the window*) I'm not likely to overlook anything concerning Miss Dale.
TOM. She was only a secretary, wasn't she?

(ROBERT *and* FARROW *turn to face Tom. There is a brief pause*)

FARROW. I'm going back to the village. Anyone want a lift?
ROBERT. I'll go with you if you don't mind.
FARROW. Hammond?
TOM. No, thanks. Actually I dropped in to ask Esmeralda and Bob up to my place on Saturday night. I've a couple of old Army friends staying the week-end. I was thinking of a small party.
ESMERALDA. How nice!
TOM. You'll come, then?
ESMERALDA. We can't. We've a long-standing date. A happy event.
TOM. Happy event?
ESMERALDA. Our wedding anniversary.
ROBERT (*to Esmeralda*) I must say I'm in a perfect mood for parties.
ESMERALDA (*rising and moving* R *of the desk*) I've already asked the Howards to come, and the Craigs, and Leslie Booth. (*To Farrow*) And you, Dick. It's only for a drink. At nine o'clock we'd planned to go to the *Clifton* for dancing. Of course we shan't do that now. (*To Tom*) You could bring your friends here.
TOM. I wouldn't do that. They're a bunch of rowdies. Some other time. Which anniversary is it?
ROBERT. Our tenth.
ESMERALDA. Won't it be wonderful when we celebrate our diamond wedding? I'd like a diamond bracelet.
FARROW. You have a diamond bracelet. I've seen it.
ESMERALDA. Yes. Dick, have a drink before you go.
FARROW. No, thanks. I can't stay.
ESMERALDA. Sherry, Robert?

(ROBERT *shakes his head*)

Tom?
TOM. A very small whisky, if you don't mind.
ESMERALDA. Help yourself.

(Tom *crosses to the cupboard down* L, *pours a drink for himself, then stands by the piano*)

(*She crosses to Farrow*) Don't be later than eight on Saturday, Dick.
FARROW. I'll remember.
ESMERALDA. You *will* come, won't you? I'm relying on you.
FARROW. Of course.

(*The cries of the gulls are heard*)

ESMERALDA. Good!
ROBERT (*hesitating by the window; to Tom*) You're staying?
TOM. To finish my whisky. With your permission, of course.
ROBERT. Oh, yes—of course.

(ESMERALDA *and* FARROW *stand together outside the door up* C. ROBERT *crosses to the radiogram, goes down on his knees and opens one door of the record cupboard. He takes out a record, puts it on the floor beside him, fiddles in the cupboard for a moment, then pushes the door to, but does not close it entirely. He picks up the record and rises.* FARROW *comes into the room*)

FARROW. Are you coming, Robert?
ROBERT (*crossing to the door up* C) Yes. I promised to lend this *Clair de Lune* to Russell Craig.

(FARROW *and* ROBERT *exit up* C. ESMERALDA *comes into the room and closes the door*)

ESMERALDA (*moving below the piano*) I didn't make it too obvious, did I—making sure he'll be here?
TOM (*moving to the cupboard down* L *and pouring a drink for Esmeralda*) You had to make sure he didn't give it a miss.
ESMERALDA. Yes. It's rather good, isn't it?

(*The sounds of a car departing are heard*)

TOM. What?
ESMERALDA. Our plan. Was it mine or yours?
TOM (*handing the drink to Esmeralda*) A little of each.
ESMERALDA. I think it's rather cute. Robert wanted me out of the way, didn't he? He gave himself a perfect alibi, and Marion undertook the actual job. Unfortunately they made a mistake.
TOM (*crossing to the desk*) Yes. They made a mistake. (*He puts his glass on the desk*)
ESMERALDA. It's poetic justice, Tom.
TOM. I don't know anything about poetry.
ESMERALDA. Then let's say it's justice. We turn the tables on them. Robert used Dick Farrow as his alibi. You have to give him credit for that. You can't go much higher than Scotland Yard. That's why we're going to do the same thing.
TOM (*moving to* R *of her*) It'd better be more successful.

ESMERALDA. Don't you think it will be?

TOM. I think maybe you've invited too many people. As soon as it happens, Craig and Howard will rush outside to make heroes of themselves.

ESMERALDA. They won't be here.

TOM. You invited them. You said so.

ESMERALDA. On Saturday I shall have a headache. I shall ring up and put them off.

TOM. That's smart. There'll only be Farrow.

ESMERALDA. And Leslie Booth. He's never moved more than twenty-five yards in his life.

TOM. That's beautiful. The only running he'll do is up and down the piano keys. Maybe that's an idea. Get him to play something loud on the piano. Then they won't hear—the shot.

ESMERALDA. Don't worry about that.

TOM. Exactly nine o'clock. That's the time it's got to be. Dead on nine.

ESMERALDA (*impressed by the double meaning*) Dead on nine o'clock. Dead on nine.

TOM (*moving to the window*) Yes. I leave my pals in the house with a couple of girls and a few bottles of gin, then I say I'm going out to the stockyard—twenty minutes will see our little job through—they won't even know I wasn't there all the time.

ESMERALDA (*moving above the desk chair*) You won't need an alibi; but it's best to be careful.

TOM (*moving to R of Esmeralda*) Even if Farrow suspects me he can't be sure. It would only be circumstantial evidence, and for that you've got to prove motive. I haven't a motive.

ESMERALDA (*smiling*) Haven't you?

TOM. Sure—but who's to know?

ESMERALDA. Just you and I—(*shrewdly*) or is there anyone else? I don't know very much about you, do I?

(TOM *moves to the sofa and sits*)

Your private life—the people you talk to—the women you know. (*She puts her glass on the desk*)

TOM. There was a girl . . .

ESMERALDA (*moving to R of the sofa*) Does she know about me?

TOM. Don't worry—she's all right. She knows I danced a few times with you.

ESMERALDA. What else?

TOM (*facing her*) Nothing—as a matter of fact I said you were keen on me, and I was sort of . . .

ESMERALDA. Being polite?

TOM. Yes. I never told her I was interested. I put her off.

ESMERALDA. Who is she?

TOM. Sheila Ryan.

ESMERALDA (*turning away*) I don't know her.

TOM (*rising and standing behind Esmeralda*) She's all right—forget about it. Concentrate on one thing. At nine o'clock you've got to have him standing there in front of the window. Can you do it?
ESMERALDA. I shall do it.
TOM. No mistakes.
ESMERALDA (*moving to the window*) He'll be there. You'll see him all right. You won't be able to miss him.
TOM (*moving to L of the window*) I won't miss him. From that window to the lane is fifteen yards. I don't miss from fifteen yards.
ESMERALDA. Farrow's the only danger. He'll act automatically. He'll start running straight out of the house in your direction.
TOM. I don't think he will. I think he'll go straight to Robert to see if he's alive or dead. Ten seconds after I fire the shot I'll be across the lane and thirty or forty yards away. Don't worry! I can take care of myself.
ESMERALDA. Then that's that.
TOM. Sure it is. We've got it straight, haven't we? You just have to take care of one thing. At nine o'clock exactly—you get him over to that window. From there on it's up to me.
ESMERALDA. And the alibi is perfect.
TOM. Perfect. (*He embraces and kisses her*)

(*The cries of the gulls are heard and continue until the end of the scene*)

ESMERALDA. You'd better go now.
TOM (*moving to the door up* C) I'm going. (*He opens the door*) We don't want anyone to figure out I've got a motive after all. Till tomorrow night.
ESMERALDA (*throwing him a kiss*) Tomorrow night.

(TOM *exits up* C, *but re-enters immediately*)

TOM. He's back already.
ESMERALDA. Robert?

(TOM *nods, moves to the desk and picks up his glass.*
ROBERT *enters up* C. *He carries the record. He stands for a moment looking first at Tom, then at Esmeralda*)

(*To Robert*) What's the matter? I thought you were going into the village.
ROBERT. I was.
ESMERALDA. Why didn't you?
ROBERT (*moving to the table* LC) I changed my mind.
ESMERALDA. Oh!
ROBERT. The police sergeant was on his way up here to find Farrow. So I came back. They've gone along the coast road to

Summerdale. (*He pauses*) Aren't you going to ask me why? (*He puts the record on the table* LC)
TOM. All right. Why?
ROBERT. They found Marion's body. It was washed up on the rocks.
TOM (*moving up* C) That's—terrible.
ROBERT. Yes, isn't it? (*He moves towards Tom, almost trembling with rage*)

(TOM *backs to the wall* R *of the door up* C)

Get out, Hammond! Get out of my house.
TOM. Now wait a minute . . .
ROBERT (*grabbing Tom by the neck*) Get out!
ESMERALDA (*quietly*) Robert, I've lost my diamond bracelet.

(ROBERT *looks at Esmeralda*)

Would you like to tell the police where it is?

CURTAIN

ACT III

Scene 1

Scene—*The same. The next morning.*

When the Curtain *rises,* Robert *is seated at the desk, facing* R. Esmeralda *is seated in the easy chair above the fireplace.* Farrow *is seated on the sofa. His attitude is restrained and undramatic.*

Esmeralda. This throws an entirely different light on the matter, I suppose?
Farrow. Well, no—not a different light. We're still pretty much in the dark. But at least we know now that she died, and how she died.
Robert. Yes, we know now.
Farrow. It puts me in an awfully difficult position with you, you know. You're my friends. (*Awkwardly*) I'm an uncomfortable sandwich between you and Lewis.
Robert. Why?
Esmeralda. Does he suspect us?
Farrow. He suspects everybody. When the finger points at no-one in particular, it points at everyone in general. And she was Robert's secretary.
Robert. Does that involve me?
Farrow. It affects you, Robert. It affects everybody she knew.
Esmeralda. She knew me.
Robert. And you, Farrow. And Hammond. And a lot of other people for that matter.
Farrow. Lewis is thorough. He asked me to compile a list of all the people with whom she came in contact——
Esmeralda. Tom Hammond scarcely knew her.
Farrow. —however remotely.
Esmeralda. I see.
Farrow. He's got to question everybody. It's a process of elimination. Eliminate the chaff and you finish up with the wheat. He will question you both again.
Robert. What answers will he hope to get?
Farrow. He'll ask you about firearms, of course.
Robert. What about them?
Farrow. He'll want to know if you keep a gun.
Robert. I don't.
Farrow. Marion was shot. Three times. Whoever did it used a revolver—the sort that was issued to certain Army officers during the war.
Robert. I was an Army officer during the war.

FARROW (*casually*) Oh! Yes.
ROBERT. I was not issued with a revolver.
FARROW. He will ask you as a matter of routine.
ROBERT (*rising*) Or are you doing the questioning for him?
FARROW. I didn't ask a question, Robert. You answered, but I didn't ask you.
ROBERT. I'm sorry.
FARROW. Actually he'd be furious if he thought I was interfering in any way.
ROBERT. I shall give him the same answer I gave you. There isn't a gun in the house.
ESMERALDA (*quietly*) That isn't quite true, Robert. There is a revolver in the house.
ROBERT (*aghast*) What did you say?
ESMERALDA. I have one.
FARROW. You have one?
ESMERALDA. I'm afraid so. It's a véry innocent revolver. But nevertheless, it exists.
FARROW. May I see it?
ESMERALDA (*rising*) Of course.

(ESMERALDA *exits* R. FARROW *and* ROBERT *are silent until she returns*. FARROW *rises and moves up* R *of the desk*. ROBERT *moves to* L *of the desk*.

ESMERALDA *re-enters. She carries the Luger which she hands to Farrow*)

It hasn't been used. (*She sits in the easy chair above the fireplace*)
FARROW. It's a Luger.
ROBERT (*surprised*) A Luger?
FARROW. Yes. (*He breaks the gun and examines the magazine*)
ESMERALDA. I'm afraid I haven't a licence for it.
FARROW. It's fully loaded. Have you ever fired it?
ESMERALDA. Heavens, no! I suppose you want to know why I have it? Well, it's pretty isolated here. One night I thought I heard voices outside my window. I couldn't sleep for thinking of it. Robert didn't seem concerned when I told him.
ROBERT. I don't remember.
ESMERALDA. But I mentioned it to someone else—a friend— I'd rather not say who—and he said I ought to keep a revolver by my bedside. He gave me that.
ROBERT. May I ask who he was?
ESMERALDA. He has no more to do with this affair than I have. Under the circumstances I'm afraid I've got to protect him.
ROBERT. I see.
FARROW. Well, we know this didn't kill her. (*To Esmeralda*) Are you sure Robert didn't know you had a gun?
ESMERALDA. No. He certainly did not.
ROBERT (*moving down* C; *to Farrow*) Why do you ask if I knew?

FARROW. I wondered.
ROBERT. I already told you I didn't know there was such a thing in the house. I don't see why on earth the official mind should suspect me of telling lies.
FARROW. I didn't say so.
ROBERT. I resent your casual attitude. Offhand insinuations. (*He moves up* C)
FARROW. Until we discover a motive, we've no reason to suspect anybody.
ROBERT (*moving down* L) So it isn't a great compliment not to be suspected, is it?
FARROW. The first enquiries, obviously, have to be directed at the people we know she knew. She was your secretary, Robert.
ROBERT (*moving up* C) She didn't confide in me.
FARROW. We know that on the night she died, she was last seen by her aunt at ten o'clock. At that time they went to bed. Next morning she was missing. She may have gone to meet somebody.
ROBERT. At six o'clock in the morning?
FARROW. Possibly.
ROBERT. I never left your house. But I can't prove it. She could have met me by appointment, and I could have . . . (*He moves to* L *of Farrow*) Or perhaps I tapped on her bedroom window and invited her to join me. Why don't you say it?
FARROW. You said it. I didn't.
ROBERT. Because it's going through your mind. Deny it if you can.
FARROW. I didn't come here to deny hysterical outbursts.
ROBERT. Of course not. I'm—sorry. (*He gives a little laugh and turns to Esmeralda*) It's rather funny, isn't it? They think I might have killed her.
ESMERALDA. What are you talking about?
ROBERT (*moving below the piano*) Nothing. Nothing at all.
FARROW. There may be a boy friend we don't know about. He may be the party we're seeking.
ESMERALDA. Why should he kill her?
FARROW. Oh, these things happen. A lover who's suddenly grown tired. A married man who's frightened in case his wife gets to hear about it. There are several variations on the theme.
ESMERALDA (*rising and moving to* R *of the desk*) It's all rather alarming. (*She indicates the Luger*) What are you going to do with my . . .?
FARROW. I'd better take care of it, hadn't I? (*He pockets the gun*)
ESMERALDA. I'm dreadfully sorry about not having a licence. Will they be very cross?
FARROW. You might make them less cross, Esmeralda, by telling Inspector Lewis the name of the person who gave it to you.

(ESMERALDA *turns away to the fireplace*)

It's the other gun he's anxious about. The one that fired the three shots that killed her. Three bullets. Whoever did it must have been very vindictive. Three bullets from such close range.

ROBERT. And if you find the gun you can find the person who used it.

FARROW. I think so.

ROBERT. And your case would be solved.

FARROW. Yes. (*He pauses and moves* C) I talk too much. As a friend of the family I'd hoped to act as a sort of buffer between you and Lewis.

ESMERALDA. We shouldn't want you to step on the Inspector's toes on our behalf. Should we, Robert? (*To Farrow*) By the way, this evening . . .

FARROW. Yes?

ESMERALDA. Under the circumstances I shall call off the party. I can put everyone off except Leslie. He isn't on the phone.

FARROW (*moving to the door up* C) Very well.

ESMERALDA. But *you* must still come, Dick.

FARROW. I must?

ROBERT (*bitterly*) Let's eat, drink and be merry.

ESMERALDA. Hardly merry. But, at least, it'll be brighter than sitting here, by ourselves, to brood over things.

ROBERT. Amen.

ESMERALDA (*moving above the desk*) So you will come, won't you, Dick?

(FARROW *looks at his watch*)

See you about eight o'clock.

FARROW. I'll remember. Well, I must be trotting along to Hammond's.

ESMERALDA (*surprised*) Why?

FARROW (*surprised at her surprise*) He asked me to.

ESMERALDA. Oh!

FARROW. He has some old Army friends staying the week-end. I promised to call in to meet them. Does it surprise you?

ESMERALDA. I—didn't know you were so friendly.

FARROW. We're not. I don't know why he asked me. Still, there it is. He did. (*He hesitates at the door. To Robert*) By the way, could you make me a loan? My fishing tackle's in a dreadful mess. Have you anything you could lend me?

ROBERT (*crossing to the window table*) Of course. (*He indicates several reels of fishing line on the table*) Will any of this do?

(FARROW *moves to the window table and selects a reel*)

FARROW. Yes, this will do splendidly. It's very kind of you. (*He moves to the door up* C) See you tonight.

(FARROW *exits up* C)

ESMERALDA (*thoughtfully*) Yes.
ROBERT (*turning to Esmeralda*) Where did you get that gun?
ESMERALDA. Which gun, Robert? There were two, weren't there?
ROBERT. Where did you get it?
ESMERALDA. Mr Farrow says it's a Luger. Had you seen it before, Robert?
ROBERT. Hammond helped you, didn't he?
ESMERALDA. I asked you a question, Robert.
ROBERT. I asked you a question, too, but you needn't answer. He took the boat out and he—got rid of—Marion.
ESMERALDA (*moving above the desk*) But how imaginative you are.
ROBERT (*moving to R of Esmeralda*) And where's the other gun, Esmeralda?
ESMERALDA (*sitting in the desk chair*) I gave it to Farrow.
ROBERT (*moving RC*) Please don't try to be funny. The gun that killed her wasn't a Luger. You had another, hadn't you? The one you used. And you were clever. You kept the Luger to show to Farrow.
ESMERALDA. I hope he admired my honesty.
ROBERT. And the joke is, he thinks I did it.
ESMERALDA. He made a mess of your alibi, didn't he? Robert, what became of my bracelet?
ROBERT (*crossing to R of the piano*) I don't know anything about it.
ESMERALDA. It's the only present you ever bought me. I remember so well that day I gave you the money for it. I do hope you did not destroy it.
ROBERT. I know no more about it than you know about the other gun. Shall we let it go at that? (*He pauses*) You heard what Farrow said. If they find it, they find the killer.
ESMERALDA. Yes.
ROBERT. Did Hammond get rid of it?

(*The cries of the gulls are heard*)

ESMERALDA. Wouldn't you like to know, Robert?
ROBERT (*moving close to her; angrily*) Yes, I would like to know.
ESMERALDA. You've pieced everything together so brilliantly. Surely you're not going to be beaten by the last piece in the jig-saw?
ROBERT. I'll get even with you, Esmeralda. Both of you.

(ROBERT *turns and exits up* C. ESMERALDA *rises, considers a moment, moves to the door up* C, *glances off, then goes to the telephone, lifts the receiver and dials a number*)

ESMERALDA (*into the telephone*) Who is that? . . . Tom! Farrow's on his way up there to see you. Did you invite him? . . .

Then it's all right . . . Yes . . . No mistakes. He's coming here tonight. About eight . . . (*She glances towards the door up* C. *Loudly*) Yes, all right. Good-bye. (*She replaces the receiver, lifts it again and dials another number. Into the telephone*) May Howard? . . . Esmeralda here . . . I'm sorry to do this, May, but I'm putting you off tonight. I know you'll understand. With this trouble about Robert's secretary . . . I knew you'd agree . . . I wonder if I can ask you a favour? . . . Would you ring Russell and Helen and explain to them? . . . Thank you very much . . . Bye-bye. (*She replaces the receiver*)

(ROBERT *enters up* C *and moves to* R *of the piano*)

ROBERT. Who was that?

ESMERALDA. I just phoned the Craigs and the Howards. I cancelled tonight. I can't put Leslie Booth off. There'll just be four of us. Would you like coffee? It might steady your nerves.

ROBERT (*smiling*) Yes, Esmeralda. Let's both steady our nerves.

CURTAIN

SCENE 2

SCENE—*The same. Evening of the same day.*

When the CURTAIN *rises, it is eight-fifty. The window and blinds are open; it is dark outside and the room is well lighted. The table* LC *has been removed and the easy chair* LC *is now below the piano. Drinks are set out on the window table.* ROBERT *is seated in the easy chair below the piano.* ESMERALDA, *glass in hand, is standing by the fireplace.* LESLIE BOOTH, *a personable young man, is seated playing the piano. His music is soft and sensuous. He has a glass on top of the piano. Throughout this scene,* ROBERT *is assured,* ESMERALDA *nervous. After a moment,* ESMERALDA, *glass in hand, crosses to the door up* C, *opens it and glances out.*

ROBERT (*impatiently*) For heaven's sake! What's the matter with you?

ESMERALDA (*closing the door*) I thought I heard him.

ROBERT. He'll come.

ESMERALDA (*moving above the desk*) He said he'd be here at eight.

ROBERT. Does it matter very much? Eight—nine—or ten, for that matter. The night's young.

ESMERALDA. I suppose you're right.

ROBERT. You're behaving curiously, Esmeralda.

ESMERALDA (*crossing below the sofa to the fireplace*) I don't think so.

ROBERT. Ah, but you are.

ESMERALDA. You must excuse me if my nerves are somewhat on edge.
ROBERT. I find that easy to understand. But I can't appreciate that Farrow's being here will calm them.
ESMERALDA. Perhaps not.
ROBERT. He has the opposite effect on me.

(LESLIE *stops playing, rises and picks up his glass*)

ESMERALDA. Please don't stop, Leslie.
LESLIE (*moving* C) I always stop when my glass is empty.
ROBERT (*rising*) I'm so sorry. (*He takes the glass from Leslie and crosses to the window table*) Will you go on playing if I give you another drink? (*He pours a gin and Dubonnet for Leslie*)
LESLIE. Oh, yes. Didn't you say the Howards were coming?
ESMERALDA. I put them off. A party didn't seem quite the thing.
LESLIE. I see. I'm glad the Howards aren't coming. May invariably wants to sing. I always think you've never really died until you've heard her sing.
ROBERT (*crossing and giving Leslie the drink*) Gin and Dubonnet. Now do we hear more music? Play something of your own.
LESLIE. Oh, yes. (*He puts his glass on the piano, sits and improvises softly on the melody of "Esmeralda"*)
ROBERT (*crossing to the window table; to Esmeralda*) Why are the drinks over here tonight? (*He pours a drink for himself*)
ESMERALDA. Why not? (*She puts her glass on the mantelpiece*)
ROBERT. No reason, I suppose. (*To Leslie*) Women have a passion for moving furniture about.

(FARROW *enters up* C)

FARROW. Hello. May I let myself in? (*He crosses to* R *of the sofa*)
ESMERALDA. Oh, there you are.
FARROW. Good evening, Esmeralda.
ESMERALDA. I thought you'd forgotten.
ROBERT. But how could he, Esmeralda? You reminded him at least twelve times.
ESMERALDA. I'm sure I didn't. Dick, you know Leslie Booth.
FARROW. Hello, Leslie.

(LESLIE *winks at Farrow*)

ROBERT. What'll it be? Gin and something? Whisky?
FARROW (*sitting on the sofa*) Whisky, if I may.
ROBERT (*pouring a drink for Farrow*) Whisky it is. My wife has had the brilliant idea of putting the drinks in front of the window. Soda?
FARROW. No, water please.
ROBERT. I'm practically spotlighted to anybody who might be

passing outside. (*He takes the drink and hands it to Farrow*) I like that tune, Leslie. What is it?

LESLIE. It's called *Esmeralda*. (*To* ESMERALDA) In your honour.

(ROBERT *moves up* C)

ESMERALDA. Indeed.

LESLIE. I did a rare thing today. I took exercise. I walked along the cliffs and the tune came into my head. When I was on my way back I saw Esmeralda and she provided me with a title.

ESMERALDA. You saw me?

LESLIE. On the cliffs. You were talking to Tom Hammond.

ROBERT. Oh?

ESMERALDA. Yes. I was there.

ROBERT. Were you?

ESMERALDA (*sitting in the easy chair above the fireplace; to* LESLIE) And you named the song after me?

LESLIE. May I sing it for you?

ESMERALDA. Please.

(LESLIE *sings*)

"ESMERALDA"

LESLIE.
Esmeralda, Esmeralda
Was an angel in disguise,
And the laughter danced
Like starlight in her eyes.

Esmeralda, Esmeralda
Was enchanting from the start,
And her laughter found an echo
In my heart.

Oh, the sound was like music,
Sweeter than a bell,
And I loved her not wisely,
But too well.

So I told her that I loved her
And how happy I could be,
If together we might live eternally,
And my lovely Esmeralda
Laughed at me.

ROBERT. Is Esmeralda's laughter so remarkable?

ESMERALDA. That was charming, Leslie. (*She rises and moves to the fireplace*) I appreciate the compliment.

(LESLIE *rises and bows.*
GLADYS *enters* L. *She carries a tray with a plate of sandwiches*)

GLADYS (*moving* LC) I'm sorry to intrude, ma'am. Can I bring the sandwiches in now?
ESMERALDA (*glancing at the clock*) No, Gladys, I said later.
GLADYS. Well, it's nearly nine o'clock and I thought . . .
ESMERALDA. No. You heard what I said.

(*There is an awkward pause.* LESLIE *relieves it by very gallantly hurrying to Gladys*)

LESLIE (*taking the plate of sandwiches from the tray*) Miss Fotheringhay—may I call you Rosemary?
GLADYS. My name's Gladys, sir.
LESLIE. That is why I should like to call you Rosemary. (*He moves to the piano stool, sits on it, pops a sandwich into his mouth and puts the plate on the piano*)

(GLADYS *exits* L)

ROBERT (*crossing and sitting in the easy chair* LC) Really, Esmeralda, what does it matter if the girl brings sandwiches at five minutes to nine? She has a long walk home, you know.

(LESLIE *turns to the piano and plays a few treble notes with one finger*)

(*To Leslie*) What do you call those two fellows who play Liszt's *Hungarian Rhapsody* on one piano?
LESLIE. I've no idea. (*He stops playing, swings round on the stool and faces Farrow*) Do you know what they're saying in the village?
FARROW. What about?
LESLIE. About the disappearance of Bob's secretary. They're saying the police haven't the faintest idea about it. (*He picks up his glass*)
FARROW (*rising and moving to the window table*) Are they? (*He puts his glass on the table and crosses to* C)
LESLIE. Yes. (*He drinks*)
FARROW. They may be right.
LESLIE. I suppose they're working very hard on the case. An announcement will shortly be made. I wish them luck. I liked her. (*He considers this*) And I don't like women as a rule. (*He puts his glass on the piano and moves to* L *of Farrow*) They say the police can't find the revolver that shot her.
FARROW. Do they? They seem to be well-informed.
LESLIE. Yes. Horrible things, revolvers. Do you know, apart from museums, I only once saw a revolver in my life. (*He turns to Robert*) That was Robert's.
ROBERT (*after a pause*) Mine?
LESLIE. Yes.
ROBERT. I never possessed a revolver.
LESLIE. But you showed it to me, Robert.
ROBERT. I haven't a revolver, I tell you.

LESLIE. Well, I'm sorry if I said the wrong thing, Robert.
ROBERT. Under the circumstances, it was a stupid thing to say.
LESLIE. Yes. (*He turns away*) I suppose it was. (*He sits at the piano, plays a few notes with one finger, then stops*) But I do remember quite distinctly.
ROBERT. Then you're quite mistaken. You're confusing me with someone else.
LESLIE. Oh! Well, it doesn't matter, does it? (*He drains his glass*)

(*The clock is now very close on nine o'clock*)

Robert, may I have another drink, please?
ROBERT. Help yourself.
LESLIE. Help myself? (*He rises, crosses to the window table and puts his glass on it*)
ESMERALDA (*perturbed*) Robert, surely you can do that.
ROBERT. He doesn't mind. Do you, Leslie?
ESMERALDA. You *are* the host.
ROBERT. Yes, I know.
ESMERALDA. Robert!
ROBERT (*casually*) Yes, Esmeralda?

(ESMERALDA *glances at the clock. It is almost nine o'clock*)

ESMERALDA (*crossing to Leslie and pushing him down* R) I'll do it, Leslie.
LESLIE. I'm quite capable of doing it.
ESMERALDA. Yes. Yes, I know. (*She stands* L *of Leslie*) This sherry's empty. Will you get another from the cabinet?
LESLIE. I drink gin.
ESMERALDA (*urgently*) Please, Leslie.
LESLIE (*surprised*) Yes, of course. (*He crosses to the cupboard down* L)
ROBERT. I wonder how Hammond's going on with his party.
FARROW. I imagine they're drunk by now. They're a pretty lively crowd.

(LESLIE *searches in the cupboard.* ESMERALDA *stands at the downstage end of the window*)

ROBERT (*rising and moving to* L *of Farrow*) Another? (*He takes Farrow's glass*) What was it? (*He crosses to the window table*)
FARROW. Scotch.
ROBERT. Oh, yes. (*He pours a drink for Farrow*)

(ESMERALDA, *unseen by Farrow, watches spellbound.* ROBERT, *having poured the drink, turns and stands with his back to the window*)

LESLIE. I don't like Hammond.
FARROW. No?

LESLIE. He walks into a room as if he's saying "Here I am. Look me over." Of course, women adore him. (*He looks again in the cupboard*)
ROBERT. Yes. He's quite a lady-killer. (*To Esmeralda*) Isn't he? (*He moves to Farrow and hands him the drink*) Your whisky.
LESLIE. But there isn't any sherry.
ROBERT (*moving to the window table*) The sherry isn't empty. Did you think it was?

(*The clock strikes nine*)

Esmeralda, are you all right?
ESMERALDA. Of course.
ROBERT. You're shivering.
ESMERALDA. I'm sure I'm not.
ROBERT. But you are. You look frozen. (*He turns to the window and very deliberately lowers the blind*) That's better, isn't it? (*He pours a drink for Leslie*) Your drink, Leslie.
LESLIE (*crossing to* LC) I really think I ought to be going, you know.
ROBERT. Oh, no.
LESLIE. Yes. I should, really.
ROBERT (*crossing to Leslie and giving him his drink*) I can't allow it. This is a great occasion.
LESLIE. Is it?
ROBERT. Yes. I have been married ten years to the day. Ten years of undiluted joy.
ESMERALDA. Excuse me.

(ESMERALDA *exits* R)

LESLIE. I do think, Robert, you might save us a little embarrassment.
ROBERT. I don't know what you mean.
LESLIE. I admire Esmeralda enormously.
ROBERT. But so do I. She's beautiful. She's intelligent. She's artistic. Do you know she paints? (*He indicates a watercolour on the wall*) She did this. She's extremely talented, you know.
LESLIE. You say it with your tongue in your cheek. Quite mistakenly, Robert. She's all the things you ironically say that she is.
ROBERT. She is more than that, Leslie. She is a magnificent example of her species. And the female of the species is more—(*he turns to Farrow and stands with his back to the audience*) what is it they say—than the male.
FARROW. Deadly.
ROBERT. Oh, is that it? Is the drink to your liking, Leslie?
LESLIE (*sitting on the piano stool*) Thank you, yes.

(*The telephone rings.* ROBERT *crosses to the piano.*
ESMERALDA *enters anxiously* R)

ESMERALDA (*crossing to* LC) Who is it?
ROBERT (*lifting the receiver*) I don't know. Were you expecting a call?
ESMERALDA. No.
ROBERT (*into the telephone*) Robert Leigh speaking... Who do you say?... Inspector Lewis. What can I do for you, Inspector?... Yes, he is here. Would you like a word with him?... Yes. Of course. Hold on a moment.
FARROW (*crossing and taking the receiver from Robert*) Now what's he want?

(ROBERT *crosses to* L *of the desk*)

(*Into the telephone*) Hello, Lewis. Farrow speaking... What is it?... No!... When did you hear about it?... Are you sure?... But... Good God!... Well, I'll come along if you wish... My car's outside. I'll meet you there. (*He replaces the receiver and crosses to* C) I'm afraid I've got to leave you.
ESMERALDA. What's the matter?
FARROW. Hammond's dead.

(ESMERALDA *sits in the easy chair* LC *and looks in silence at Robert*)

ROBERT. That's awful. How—what happened?
FARROW. It appears to be an accident.
ESMERALDA. Accident?
FARROW. He was found this morning at the bottom of the cliff. His neck's broken.
ROBERT. Good heavens!
FARROW. There's been a landslide.
ROBERT. Will you call back and let us know—more about it? Naturally we're upset.
FARROW (*moving up* C) I'll do that.

(FARROW *exits up* C)

LESLIE (*rising; in a hurry to go*) If you don't mind I'll push off at the same time.
ROBERT. If you insist, Leslie.
LESLIE. Yes. (*He puts his glass on the piano*) You don't mind, do you, Esmeralda? Are you all right? You're very pale.
ROBERT. I will take care of her, thank you, Leslie.
LESLIE. Yes. (*He moves to the door up* C) Thank you so much for asking me here. It was charming.

(LESLIE *exits quickly up* C)

ESMERALDA (*staring at Robert*) You did it, didn't you?
ROBERT (*sitting on the left end of the desk*) Terrible news, isn't it? These landslides are always happening, aren't they?
ESMERALDA. You did it. (*She turns away*)

ROBERT. Do you remember how appalled you were when I asked you what had happened to Marion?
ESMERALDA. That was your own doing. It was the merest chance that I happened to be on the verandah.
ROBERT. So you're coming out into the open.
ESMERALDA (*rising and moving to Robert*) We're both out in the open.
ROBERT. I gave you credit for a more fastidious choice of lover. He took her out in his boat—didn't he—and threw her lifeless body in the sea. She was shot three times.
ESMERALDA. Yes. Three times.
ROBERT. And her gun hadn't been fired.
ESMERALDA. You mean—your gun hadn't been fired.
ROBERT. You met Hammond by the cliff, didn't you? Leslie saw you. And so did I.
ESMERALDA. You followed me?
ROBERT. I was there. Unlike you, I was not seen by anyone else. How amusing of you, Esmeralda, to imagine I should die a sudden death whilst pouring a drink.
ESMERALDA. Indeed?
ROBERT. I rarely enjoyed myself so much. To see your frantic efforts to manoeuvre your night-club piano-player away from the window. To see you nervously pacing up to the door. It was such a colossal waste of nervous energy. Hammond wasn't there after all, was he?
ESMERALDA. You're very clever, Robert.
ROBERT. I knew you were up to something when he stayed behind with you and let me leave with Farrow. So I overheard your conversation. I hadn't known you could be so passionate—or dangerous. (*He rises, crosses to the radiogram, takes a small tape-record from the record cupboard, stands it on top and switches it on*)

(*The recorder plays back an excerpt from Esmeralda's conversation with Tom in Act II, Scene 2*)

ESMERALDA (*from the recorder*) He'll be there. You'll see him all right. You won't be able to miss him.
TOM (*from the recorder*) I won't miss him. From that window to the lane is fifteen yards. I don't miss from fifteen yards.
ESMERALDA (*from the recorder*) Farrow's the only danger. He'll act automatically. He'll start running straight out of the house in your direction.
TOM (*from the recorder*) I don't think he will. I think he'll go straight to Robert to see if he's alive or dead.

(ROBERT *switches off the recorder*)

ESMERALDA. So you followed me, and waited until I left him.
ROBERT. Did I? (*He replaces the recorder in the cupboard*)
ESMERALDA. Then what did you do? Perhaps you called to him

and stood beside him and talked to him. Or did you point to a seagull—or a ship—and when he wasn't looking . . .

ROBERT (*moving to* L *of Esmeralda*) This is scandalous talk. There has been an accident.

ESMERALDA. And then you kicked a few stones loose and the edge caved in. (*She crosses below the sofa to* R *of the desk*) How brave of you, Robert. How very brave!

ROBERT. Was he going to be brave—dead on nine o'clock?

ESMERALDA (*turning to the fireplace*) I'm not ashamed. You sent *her* to kill me.

ROBERT (*moving* C) I loved her. She loved me. You could have avoided all this. You wouldn't let me go and—and it led to this.

ESMERALDA. Yes. It led to this. I didn't know you'd do that. I couldn't believe you'd try to kill me. I hadn't the wit to realize you might hire someone to do it for you.

ROBERT. She wasn't for hire.

(*There is a pause*)

ESMERALDA (*turning and moving to* R *of the desk*) Are we going on in perpetual fear of each other?

ROBERT. You needn't be afraid. Your secret's safe with me. I can ruin you, but only if I destroy myself.

ESMERALDA. And *vice versa*.

ROBERT. Yes.

ESMERALDA. How I hate you, Robert.

ROBERT. Need I comment on that, Esmeralda? (*He moves* LC *and lights a cigarette*)

(FARROW *enters up* C)

Hello! Come in.

FARROW (*moving* C) Thank you.

ROBERT. Will you have a drink?

FARROW. No, thank you. I came straight back.

ESMERALDA (*sitting on the sofa*) Yes?

ROBERT. What had happened?

FARROW. He fell—or he was pushed—over the edge of the cliff.

ROBERT. Pushed? Oh, come now!

FARROW. It might have been an accident. These things do happen, of course. But would you like to hear my unofficial opinion?

ROBERT. Naturally.

FARROW. I don't believe for one moment that it was an accident.

ROBERT. You don't?

FARROW. No. Inspector Lewis has an idea that it links up with Marion Dale's death. Hammond went out with his boat the night she disappeared.

ESMERALDA. He often went out at night.

FARROW. Yes. I know he did.
ESMERALDA. Lewis has no reason to connect him with her.
FARROW. Hammond had women all over the district. I suppose he was attractive in a rugged sort of way. Perhaps Marion Dale found him so.
ESMERALDA. Nonsense!
FARROW. Really? Why?
ESMERALDA. Oh, I suppose it's possible . . .
ROBERT. I don't see the connexion.
FARROW. Perhaps Hammond got rid of her because she was becoming a nuisance.
ROBERT. And then what?
FARROW. Another of his women was jealous and got rid of him.
ESMERALDA. That's pure theorizing.
FARROW. I agree. When the Inspector has no facts to work on, he falls back on theory.
ROBERT. Who found the body?
FARROW. One of the cowmen.
ROBERT (*casually*) Could he have done it?
FARROW. Yes. But he didn't.
ESMERALDA. You sound as if you know who did.
FARROW. I do.
ESMERALDA. You do?
FARROW (*sitting in the desk chair*) Perhaps I exaggerate. Let's say I've narrowed the field considerably. It couldn't have been the cowman. For one thing, he hadn't an alibi.
ROBERT. I don't follow you.
FARROW. The man who finds the body is obviously the first person you'd say had the opportunity to be responsible for the murder.
ROBERT. You say murder.
FARROW. Yes.
ROBERT. Can you prove it?
FARROW. Do you know, I doubt if I ever could. You see, there's no motive I could actually *prove*.
ROBERT. Do you mean you *know* the motive?
FARROW. Yes. In general, yes. In detail, no. There were no witnesses. I only know of one person who was within a hundred yards of the cliff during that day.
ROBERT (*sitting on the piano stool*) Who was that? (*He stubs out his cigarette in the ashtray on the piano*)
FARROW. Esmeralda.
ESMERALDA. Me?
FARROW. Weren't you?
ESMERALDA. I often walk along the cliffs.
FARROW. You were there with Hammond. Leslie Booth saw you there.
ESMERALDA. Are you—are you suggesting that I know about it?

FARROW. No, Esmeralda. Nothing of the kind. I'm only pointing out that you, like the cowman, have not got an alibi to prove your innocence. I think the person who *was* there—and did it—would have an alibi to prove he *wasn't* there and couldn't have done it. Like myself, for instance. Or even Robert here.

ROBERT. Surely it isn't only the guilty who have an alibi?

FARROW. Well, now, you've got a point there.

ROBERT (*rising and moving* LC) I think I have.

FARROW. I'm in rather a spot, as a matter of fact. In my experience it's unique. Shall I tell you about it?

ROBERT. Please do.

FARROW. I'm afraid you won't like it.

ROBERT. I can't imagine why not.

FARROW. Because what I have to say won't be complimentary. It means the end of our friendship.

ROBERT (*moving to the piano*) Go on.

FARROW (*swinging his chair to face Robert*) I'm going to make an accusation.

ROBERT. Let's hope you can prove it.

FARROW. I can't.

ROBERT. So it amounts to guesswork?

FARROW. I don't call it guesswork.

ROBERT. What's your name for it?

FARROW. Deduction.

ROBERT. I must warn you that anything you say may be taken down and used as evidence against you. I refer to the suit for defamation of character which I shall bring against you.

FARROW. You won't sue for defamation of character, Robert. I feel quite safe there.

ROBERT. All right. Go on.

FARROW. Very well. Robert, I think Marion Dale was your mistress.

ROBERT. Indeed?

FARROW. Yes.

ROBERT. And when I spent the night at your house, I suppose I slipped out whilst you were asleep and quietly murdered her. That's what you implied this morning.

FARROW. I'm glad you mentioned that. It's rather amusing. I'll tell you why later. No, I don't think you did that, Robert.

ROBERT. Thank you.

FARROW. Why did Marion leave her house that night? Where did she go? Did she—I wonder—come here? Did she, in fact, come here to put an end to Esmeralda?

ROBERT. Do you think she did?

FARROW. Esmeralda wouldn't give you a divorce. You had to find some way of getting rid of her. No-one would suspect Marion Dale. And you had an alibi. You were with me.

ROBERT. It wasn't my idea to go with you. It was yours.

FARROW (*smiling*) Yes. Wasn't it! That was rather clever.
ROBERT. Go on. What happened next?
FARROW. Somehow the plan went wrong. Marion was at the receiving end. Esmeralda and Hammond were lovers. Perhaps he was here—when you were away.
ESMERALDA (*rising*) That isn't true.
FARROW. Isn't it?
ESMERALDA. No.
FARROW. Well, I accept the correction. He wasn't here. So you sent for him.
ESMERALDA. No.
FARROW. I think so. I think he drove her down to the beach, took her out to sea and got rid of her that way.
ESMERALDA } (*together*) { You're making it all up.
ROBERT   { Pure invention!

(ESMERALDA *turns to the fireplace*)

FARROW. But it's true, isn't it?
ROBERT. What it amounts to is circumstantial evidence based on imagined circumstances. It doesn't hold water. Nobody would accept it.
FARROW. That's true also. Shall I go on?
ROBERT (*moving* LC) Yes, let's hear about Hammond's death. Esmeralda was his mistress. She met him on the cliffs. Why did she kill him? Jealousy? Or did I do it?
FARROW. Yes, Robert, you did.
ROBERT (*moving down* L) Proof! Proof! (*He stands with his back to the audience*) Give me proof. Where's my motive? At least you must find a motive. (*He moves* LC)
FARROW. Revenge, perhaps. Esmeralda had stolen a march over you. What's more natural—to you, I mean—than to even things up by destroying Hammond?
ROBERT. Excellent. (*He crosses above Farrow to* R *of the desk. To Esmeralda*) You haven't got an alibi for Hammond's death so, of course, to our Mr Farrow, I'm the guilty one. The finger points one way so no one searches in the opposite direction.
FARROW. Am I near the truth?
ROBERT. That Esmeralda killed Marion—and that I killed Hammond? Does it satisfy you? Does everything dovetail?
FARROW. Oh, yes.
ROBERT. Except the minor detail of your not having the slightest evidence to support one word of the fantastic rigmarole.
FARROW. It would be difficult to prove.
ROBERT. Wouldn't it now! Oh, wouldn't it! Can you imagine Counsel for the Prosecution: "The evidence we bring has no foundation in fact, m'lud. It is the wild imaginings of Mr Richard Farrow, the eminent criminologist, but it is so interesting we felt you ought not to be deprived of the pleasure of hearing

it." You were right, Farrow—our friendship is at an end. You may leave as soon as you please.

FARROW. I don't propose to stay much longer.

ROBERT. I'm delighted to hear it.

FARROW. But do you really imagine you're going to get away scot-free?

ESMERALDA. What do you mean? (*She moves to Robert*) He hates us. Why does he hate us both like this?

ROBERT. Yes. Why? Why do you?

FARROW (*rising and moving* C) I don't like to see a fish get off the hook.

ROBERT. It goes deeper than that.

FARROW. Does it?

ROBERT (*moving above the desk*) It was Marion. Yes—Marion.

ESMERALDA. What do you mean?

ROBERT. How stupid of me. You were interested in her.

ESMERALDA (*to Farrow*) Is that true?

FARROW (*moving to the piano*) I liked her.

ROBERT. You did more than that. Your eyes followed her about. You asked her to meet you?

FARROW. Yes, I did.

ROBERT. And she wouldn't.

FARROW. No.

ROBERT. She happened to prefer me, and you hated me for it. And that's the way it was.

FARROW. No. no. That won't do. It really won't, you know. I envied you, but I'd no resentment. But when she died—and when I realized that through your cowardice and stupidity she ended her life so sordidly—then I despised you. (*To Esmeralda*) And when I knew that you and that clumsy oaf destroyed her and threw her body in the sea . . . I can see everything almost as clearly as if I'd been there at the time. Her body trussed and tied ready to be dumped in the sea . . .

ROBERT. So that's why you don't want to let the fish get off the hook.

FARROW. It's more. It's why I don't intend to allow it to do so.

ROBERT. You can't do anything about it.

(FARROW *now begins to assume command of the situation. His confidence grows as theirs diminishes*)

FARROW. All right. Now I'll tell you something. It ought to amuse you, but I'm afraid it won't. It's really rather beautiful. I agree we can't find sufficient evidence that Robert murdered Hammond. It's frustrating. But Inspector Lewis has found a wonderful solution. Somehow he's got everything mixed up. He can prove everything—in reverse.

ROBERT. He can—what?

FARROW. He thinks you killed Marion Dale.

ROBERT. You know I didn't.

FARROW. Yes, but Lewis doesn't. And you did kill Hammond. In other words, you see, he's prepared to prove what is actually opposite to the truth.

ROBERT. You can't let him do that.

FARROW. Why not? If the murderer is brought to justice does it matter how we go about it?

ROBERT (*moving to* L *of the desk*) Of course it matters. It's perjury.

FARROW. Oh, no. He really believes it's you.

ROBERT. But you don't.

FARROW. It no longer concerns me. My conscience will be clear.

ROBERT. How in heaven's name can he prove I killed Marion? I didn't.

FARROW. She was going to bear your child.

ROBERT. That's not true.

FARROW. We have the police surgeon's evidence as to her condition.

(ESMERALDA *kneels on the sofa*)

ROBERT. Can Lewis also prove that I was responsible?

FARROW. He can prove that it's most improbable that you're not.

ROBERT. How?

FARROW. Marion's aunt.

ROBERT. She knows nothing.

FARROW. Really! How naïve of you! They lived under the same roof.

ROBERT. Marion wouldn't tell her.

FARROW. But she knew.

ROBERT. I don't believe it.

FARROW. You will when you hear her evidence. She knew of your affair perfectly well. She warned her niece. She knew also that you quarrelled.

ROBERT (*moving up* C) Who doesn't quarrel?

FARROW (*airily*) Oh, quite.

ROBERT (*moving to* R *of Farrow*) What's the point of all this?

FARROW. That she was about to bear your child and that you couldn't—or didn't want to—marry her. That you quarrelled. And that she was beginning to be a nuisance. And so you . . . (*He shrugs*)

ROBERT. Got rid of her? You know it's a lie.

(*There is a pause*)

FARROW. Yes, I know. But Lewis doesn't. And then, of course, there's the fishing line—that's very important.

ROBERT. What are you getting at now?

FARROW (*moving* LC) The cord that was used to tie her arms and legs together. It was fastened to rocks to keep her at the bottom of the sea.

ROBERT. What about it?

FARROW. Do you remember, I borrowed *your* fishing tackle, Robert? I'm afraid I misled you. I wanted to compare the two. They're identical.

ROBERT. I know nothing about it.

FARROW. Don't you?

ROBERT. You know damn well I don't.

FARROW. But Lewis doesn't. And would the jury? You built up an alibi against Esmeralda's death. I was it, wasn't I? She was to die early in the morning, I suppose. All right. Now, as Lewis sees it, at six o'clock my telephone rang and he, in great excitement, asked me to go round to see him. I did so. Your alibi with me ends there, and begins again at seven-thirty when I got back. Well, that's all right. Medical evidence would have shown that Esmeralda's death took place earlier than that. But what about Marion? You were staying the night with me. Inspector Lewis thinks this was your chance to arrange to meet her. You weren't to know I should leave the house. Normally I'd have been asleep and wouldn't have heard you go or come back. Half an hour, or less, was all it required. And you had an hour and a half—to kill. Do you see? You have no alibi from six a.m. until seven-thirty. You could have met her during that time, and done away with her and thrown her body into the sea. The sea has destroyed every particle of evidence as to the exact time of her death.

ROBERT. That's the dirtiest lie I ever heard.

FARROW. But he can prove it's true. And you did kill Hammond.

ESMERALDA. You have the wrong alibi, Robert.

FARROW (*moving up* C) That's amusing, isn't it, Esmeralda?

(ROBERT *moves* RC)

Shortly before Hammond's death you went to meet him. Leslie saw you with him.

ESMERALDA (*rising*) That wasn't a crime.

FARROW. But it's a fact. Amongst his papers Lewis found a part of a letter he was writing to a woman.

ESMERALDA. He never wrote to me.

FARROW. No. It was to a Miss Ryan. She'd been his light o' love. You had apparently put out the light. Lewis has seen the letter he wrote. In it Hammond told her he was trying to shake you off, but it wasn't easy.

ESMERALDA. It's fantastic!

FARROW. Yes. He was trying to shake her off, wasn't he? Hammond told Miss Ryan you were jealous of her.

ESMERALDA. He couldn't.
FARROW. But he did. He said you had money, and . . . But why bother about details. You'll hear them at the trial. Did you know he had a police record in Canada? Were you jealous of Miss Ryan?
ESMERALDA. You know better.
FARROW. Lewis doesn't . . .
ESMERALDA (*moving up* R *of the desk*) What do you mean?
FARROW. You were jealous of her. You met him on the cliff. You quarrelled over her, and in a fit of rage . . .
ESMERALDA. You know that's absurd.
FARROW. But you did kill Marion. And you were the last to see Hammond alive. I don't know all the details, but I think you planned to kill Robert tonight during the party and I think I was your alibi. Well, it was Hammond who died. You have the wrong alibi too, Esmeralda.
ESMERALDA (*moving to Robert*) You're trying to frighten me.
FARROW. I am frightening you. (*He glances at Robert*) Both of you. Because nobody can stare retribution in the face and be anything but frightened.
ROBERT. You're bluffing.
FARROW. Am I?

(ROBERT *turns his back on Farrow*)

ESMERALDA. Are you serious?
FARROW. Lewis is. He thinks it's the most open and shut case he's ever been concerned with. Isn't that amusing?
ESMERALDA (*moving to* C) But he's wrong.
FARROW. He says there's no loophole for either of you. He can prove it without a shadow of a doubt.
ESMERALDA. The wrong murder?
FARROW. But the right verdict.
ROBERT (*turning*) My God, he means it.
FARROW. Certainly.
ESMERALDA. But it's wrong.
FARROW. It's justice.
ROBERT (*to Esmeralda*) What can we do?
FARROW. Oh, you can do a lot. When Lewis takes you to court you can make an utter fool of him. You can prove he's mistaken. (*He takes a cigarette from his case*)
ESMERALDA (*bitterly*) By telling the truth.
FARROW (*picking up the lighter from the piano*) Yes, Esmeralda.
ESMERALDA. And the result will be the same.
FARROW. And the result will be the same. (*He lights his cigarette*)

ESMERALDA *starts to laugh as—*

the CURTAIN *falls*

FURNITURE AND PROPERTY PLOT

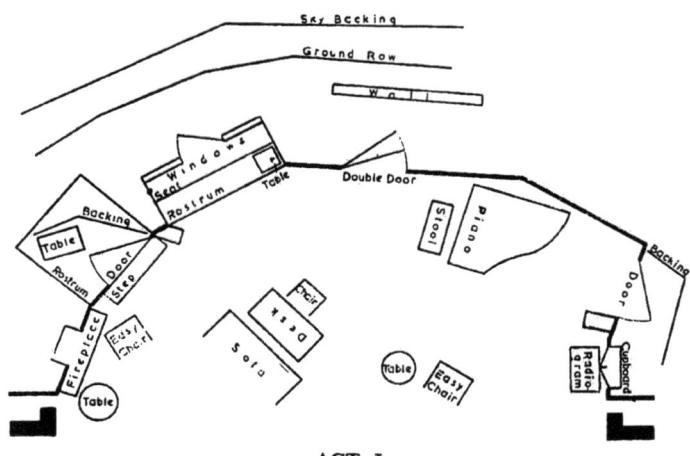

ACT I

Scene 1

On stage—Occasional table (down R). *On it:* 2 magazines
Easy chair (R). *On it:* cushion
Sofa. *On it:* cushions
Desk. *On it:* manuscript, ten pages typed, ten pages written; blotter, pen, pencil, ashtray, matches, 2 beer tankards; Robert's cigarette case with 2 cigarettes
    In drawer: Luger, spare key
Desk chair
Baby grand piano. *On it:* box with cigarettes, ashtray, matches, lighter, magazine, table-lamp, telephone
Duet stool
Radiogram. *In it:* tape recorder, 1 record
    On it: bottle of beer, opened
Easy chair (LC). *On it:* cushion
Small table (LC). *On it:* ashtray
Cupboard (down L). *In it:* bottle of whisky, syphon of soda, bottle of brandy, 6 glasses, size fifty box of cigarettes, half full, other bottles and glasses as dressing
Table (*in window*). *On it:* bowl of roses, ashtray, matches
    Under it: fishing-basket, 5 reels, coil of rope, flags
On window seat: 5 magazines, Robert's scarf
On mantelpiece: potted plant, box with cigarettes, matches, ashtray, ornamental ship, table-lamp
At L end of window: red and white buoy
On wall R of door up C: 2 fishing nets, gaff
On wall L of door up C: clock, bell, anchor, barometer
On wall L of window seat: 2 plants, lute

  On wall above cupboard: wheel
  R *of arch:* ship's starboard lamp
  L *of arch:* ship's port light
  Large zebra rug LC
  Suitable dressing for fireplace
  On wall: watercolour
  Venetian blinds
  Light switch L of door up C
  In backing R: table. *On it:* bowl of flowers

Window shut
Door up C open
Clock set at 6.30
Light fittings off

Off stage—2 trout (FARROW)
  Notebook and pencil (MARION)

Personal—ESMERALDA: handbag. *In it:* notes
  FARROW: case with cigarettes
  ROBERT: case with cigarettes, desk key
  MARION: wrist-watch

SCENE 2

Strike—Beer bottle, 2 tankards
Set—*On sofa:* Esmeralda's handbag. *In it:* compact
 Move table down R to R of sofa

Clock at 3.50
Door up C ajar
Window open
Light fittings off

Off stage—Trug basket. *In it:* gladioli (ESMERALDA)
  Vase of gladioli (MARION)
  Scarf (ESMERALDA)
  Wrap (MARION)

SCENE 3

Replace table down R
Close window blind
Clock at 2.2
Door up C, closed
Window closed
Light fittings off
Personal—ESMERALDA: coat, handbag. *In it:* door key

ACT II

SCENE 1

Clock at 10.1
Door up C closed
Window closed
Window blind closed
Light fittings off

Off stage—Holdall (ROBERT)
  Tray. *On it:* 2 cups of coffee, basin of sugar (GLADYS)
  Bunch of roses (ESMERALDA)

Personal—ROBERT: case with cigarettes, matches

Scene 2

Strike—Bunch of roses, dirty glasses, Tom's cap
Clock at 2.15
Door up c ajar
Window open
Window blind open
Light fittings off
Personal—FARROW: Marion's wrist-watch

ACT III

Scene 1

Strike—Record
Clock at 11.25
Door up c ajar
Window closed
Window blind open
Light fittings off
Off stage—Luger (ESMERALDA)
Personal—FARROW: watch

Scene 2

Strike—Table from LC
    Move chair LC to below piano
Set—*On window table:* tray with bottles of gin, whisky and Dubonnet, decanter of sherry, glass jug of water, 3 glasses
    On piano: glass, bowl of crisps
    On mantelpiece: glass
Clock at 8.50
Door up c closed
Window open
Window blind open
Light fittings on
Off stage—Tray. *On it:* plate of sandwiches (GLADYS)
Personal—ROBERT: case with cigarettes, matches
    FARROW: case with cigarettes

LIGHTING PLOT

Property Fittings Required: 2 table-lamps, 2 pairs wall-brackets (practical)
Interior. A living-room. The same scene throughout
THE MAIN ACTING AREAS ARE—up C, R, at a sofa (RC) and at easy chairs R and LC

ACT I SCENE 1 A sunny September afternoon.
THE APPARENT SOURCES OF LIGHT ARE—in daytime a window up R, and at night wall-brackets and table-lamps R and up LC

To open: Effect of bright sunshine
Strips outside doors R and L, on
Fittings off

Cue 1	ESMERALDA: "Are you coming to the party?" *Commence slow fade of lights for sunset effect*	(page 6)
Cue 2	MARION: "Darling, I do." *The lights slowly dim as the sun sets*	(page 7)
Cue 3	MARION switches on lights *Snap in table-lamps and brackets* *Bring up onstage lights*	(page 11)
Cue 4	ROBERT: ". . . like to do that." *Fade exterior lighting as night falls*	(page 12)

ACT I SCENE 2 Afternoon
To open: Effect of bright sunshine
Strips outside doors R and L, on
Fittings off

No cues

ACT I SCENE 3 Night
To open: The stage in darkness
Strips outside doors R and L, on
Fittings off
Blue floods outside window and door up C

Cue 5	ESMERALDA switches on lights *Snap in table-lamps and brackets* *Bring up onstage lights*	(page 20)
Cue 6	TOM: ". . . something about it after all." *Lightning flash*	(page 21)
Cue 7	TOM exits up C *Lightning flash*	(page 23)
Cue 8	ESMERALDA switches off lights *Snap out table-lamps and brackets* *Take out onstage lights*	(page 23)
Cue 9	ESMERALDA moves down L and closes cupboard doors *Lightning flash*	(page 23)
Cue 10	ESMERALDA exits second time *Lightning flash*	(page 23)
Cue 11	MARION enters up C *Lightning flash*	(page 23)
Cue 12	MARION exits R *Lightning flash*	(page 23)

ACT II SCENE 1 Morning

To open: The stage dimly lit
    Pale sunshine effect behind window blind and door up C
    Strips outside doors L and R, on
    Fittings off

Cue 13 GLADYS opens door up C   (page 24)
    Bring lights up to ½

Cue 14 GLADYS opens window blind   (page 24)
    Bring lights up to full

ACT II SCENE 2 Afternoon

To open: Effect of sunlight
    Strips on side doors L and R, on
    Fittings off

No cues

ACT III SCENE 1 Morning

To open: Effect of sunlight
    Strips outside doors L and R, on
    Fittings off

No cues

ACT III SCENE 2 Night

To open: Effect of sunlight
    Strips outside doors L and R, on
    Fittings off

No cues

ACT III SCENE 2 Night

To open: Blue outside window and door up C
    Strips outside doors L and R, on
    Table-lamps and brackets, on

No cues

EFFECTS PLOT

ACT I

SCENE 1

Cue 1	At rise of CURTAIN *Effect of wind and surf*	(page 1)
Cue 2	ESMERALDA: ". . . couldn't you?" *Fade surf effect*	(page 5)
Cue 3	ROBERT: "Do you understand?" *Sounds of a car departing*	(page 7)
Cue 4	MARION: "Everything depends on that." *Commence surf effect*	(page 9)
Cue 5	ROBERT: "My darling Marion, they can't." *Sounds of a car arriving and stopping*	(page 10)
Cue 6	ROBERT: "Yes, tomorrow." *Fade surf effect*	(page 12)

SCENE 2

Cue 7	At rise of CURTAIN *Effect of wind* *Telephone ringing*	(page 14)
Cue 8	MARION answers telephone *Stop telephone*	(page 14)
Cue 9	ESMERALDA *enters* R *Fade wind*	(page 14)
Cue 10	MARION: "I don't think so." *Effect of wind*	(page 16)
Cue 11	MARION: "Then you don't want him." *Fade wind*	(page 17)
Cue 12	MARION: "That isn't the case." *Effect of gulls' cries*	(page 17)
Cue 13	MARION exits *Sounds of a car arriving and stopping*	(page 18)
Cue 14	TOM: "Miss Dale?" *Fade gulls*	(page 18)
Cue 15	MARION: ". . . won't let her go." *Effect of wind*	(page 19)

SCENE 3

Cue 16	At rise of CURTAIN *Effect of wind*	(page 20)
Cue 17	ESMERALDA: ". . . to bring me home." *Fade wind*	(page 20)
Cue 18	TOM exits up C *Sounds of a car departing*	(page 23)
Cue 19	MARION *enters up* C *Sound of door creaking*	(page 23)
Cue 20	After MARION exits R *3 pistol shots*	(page 23)

ACT II

Scene 1

Cue 21	At rise of CURTAIN *Sound of car arriving and stopping*	(page 24)
Cue 22	GLADYS opens door up C *Effect of wind*	(page 24)
Cue 23	GLADYS: "I never disturb her." *Fade wind*	(page 24)
Cue 24	FARROW: "What on earth . . .?" *Effect of surf*	(page 27)
Cue 25	ESMERALDA and FARROW exit *Sound of a car starting and departing*	(page 30)
Cue 26	ROBERT: "I don't suppose so." *Telephone rings*	(page 31)
Cue 27	ROBERT answers telephone *Stop telephone*	(page 31)
Cue 28	ROBERT: "Is she all right?" *Fade surf*	(page 31)
Cue 29	GLADYS: ". . . the side of the sink." *Effect of gulls' cries*	(page 33)
Cue 30	TOM: ". . . know she's been there?" *Fade gulls*	(page 33)

Scene 2

Cue 31	ROBERT: "Now what do we do?" *Effect of car arriving and stopping*	(page 38)
Cue 32	ROBERT: ". . . hate you for it." *Effect of gulls' cries*	(page 38)
Cue 33	ESMERALDA: "I had to be sure." *Fade gulls*	(page 39)
Cue 34	FARROW: "Of course." *Effect of gulls' cries*	(page 43)
Cue 35	ESMERALDA: "It's rather good, isn't it?" *Sounds of a car departing*	(page 43)
Cue 36	ESMERALDA: ". . . made a mistake." *Fade gulls*	(page 43)
Cue 37	TOM: "Perfect." *Effect of gulls' cries. This continues until the end of the scene*	(page 45)

ACT III

Scene 1

Cue 38	ESMERALDA: ". . . revolver in the house." *Effect of wind*	(page 48)
Cue 39	FARROW: "Possibly." *Fade wind*	(page 49)
Cue 40	ROBERT: ". . . he thinks I did it." *Effect of wind*	(page 51)
Cue 41	ROBERT: ". . . get rid of it." *Effect of gulls' cries*	(page 51)

Scene 2

Cue 42	ROBERT: ". . . think it was?" *Clock strikes 9*	(page 57)
Cue 43	LESLIE: "Thank you, yes." *Telephone rings*	(page 57)
Cue 44	ROBERT answers telephone *Stop telephone*	(page 58)

www.ingramcontent.com/pod-product-compliance
Ingram Content Group UK Ltd.
Pitfield, Milton Keynes, MK11 3LW, UK
UKHW021840210426
5322IPUK00022B/390